D0110124

THE MYTH OF HAPPINESS

THE MYTH OF HAPPINESS

discovering a joy
you never thought possible

rich wagner

ZONDERVAN®

ZONDERVAN.com/
AUTHORTRACKER
follow your favorite authors

The Myth of Happiness

Copyright © 2007 by Rich Wagner

Requests for information should be addressed to:
Zondervan, *Grand Rapids, Michigan* 49530

Library of Congress Cataloging-in-Publication Data

Wagner, Richard, 1966 –
    The myth of happiness : discovering a joy you never thought possible /
Rich Wagner.
       p. cm.
    Includes bibliographical references.
    ISBN-13: 978-0-310-27487-2
    ISBN-10: 0-310-27487-7
    1. Joy – Religious aspects – Christianity. 2. Christian life. I. Title.
BV4647.J68W35   2007
248.4 – dc22

                                         2006037565

All Scripture quotations, unless otherwise indicated, are taken from the *Holy Bible, Today's New International Version*™. TNIV®. Copyright © 2001, 2005 by International Bible Society. Used by permission of Zondervan. All rights reserved.

The website addresses recommended throughout this book are offered as a resource to you. These websites are not intended in any way to be or imply an endorsement on the part of Zondervan, nor do we vouch for their content for the life of this book.

All rights reserved. No part of this publication may be reproduced, stored in a retrieval system, or transmitted in any form or by any means – electronic, mechanical, photocopy, recording, or any other – except for brief quotations in printed reviews, without the prior permission of the publisher.

Published in association with the literary agency of Alive Communications, Inc., 7680 Goddard Street, Suite 200, Colorado Springs, CO 80920.

Interior design by Beth Shagene

Printed in the United States of America

07 08 09 10 11 12 • 23 22 21 20 19 18 17 16 15 14 13 12 11 10 9 8 7 6 5 4 3 2 1

With joy — to Kimberly and the J-boys

CONTENTS

ACKNOWLEDGMENTS

In writing this book, I am deeply indebted to three heroes of mine—Oswald Chambers, C. H. Spurgeon, and C. S. Lewis. Each of these great Christian thinkers has had a profound influence in my understanding of what biblical joy is.

I was blessed to be surrounded by many "lumps of sunshine," as Spurgeon would say, who have shared their joy with me. Deepest thanks to Bruce Marciano, Mitch Lamotte, Karen Blackmer, Donovan Donaldson, Linda Goehle, Judy Benoit, Clint Frank, and John Vedoe for providing me a glimpse into what real joy looks like.

Rev. Joseph Wagner proved a great sounding board and was the primary driver behind the discussion guide. Thanks, Dad! Thanks also to Angela Scheff at Zondervan for her input on the initial draft and for challenging me to produce a better, more personal book. Many thanks to Verlyn Verbrugge for his editorial strength and keen attention to detail.

For every book I write, my wife, Kimberly, is always the first person to read my drafts and is my first line of feedback. I wouldn't know how to write anything without her 24/7 support. I thank her and my three boys, Jordan, Jared, and Justus, for their constant encouragement and prayers.

All of the personal stories in the book are true. However, in some cases, I changed the names to preserve confidentiality.

Rich Wagner
October 2006

PART 1

THIRSTY FOR MORE

CHAPTER 1

A SEMI-CHARMED LIFE

I want something else to get me through
this semi-charmed kind of life.
—Third Eye Blind, "Semi-Charmed Life"

I think I've been asleep most of my life.
—Claire Colburn, *Elizabethtown*

Thirst. Seek. Settle. For nonbelievers and believers alike, much of life in today's world can be summed up with those three verbs. When you are young and motivated, you thirst for a great career, terrific spouse, or a chance to make a difference in the world. You graduate from school, and then you spend the next few years in pursuit of that dream.

The vast majority of people, however, never reach the lofty heights that they set out for. Their career stalls. They discover they're not as talented as they thought or never got the lucky break they deserved. Even marriage and home life turn out to be a letdown. Consequently, at some point in their thirties or so, many people begin to settle; they adjust to their new less-than-perfect reality and make the best of it—for awhile.

As people approach middle age, however, something happens. A midlife crisis for some, a reawakening for others. Whatever you call it, many people wake up from their stalled life and begin to thirst again. Through career changes, divorces, and fancy toys, people try once more to find happiness while there is still time left to enjoy it. These rekindled fires rarely last, however. They fizzle out in time, and people find themselves resigning once more, coasting into retirement.

When I look at unbelievers around me, I can easily spot this cycle in their lives. I hear rumors that my depressed, middle-aged neighbor is turning into an alcoholic. In his eyes, I see shades of the doomed soul in *The Screwtape Letters* who said, "I now see that I spent most of my life in doing *neither* what I ought *nor* what I liked." I spot the same dead-end thinking when I talk with my friend Mike, who recently jumped ship, leaving his wife and family in a desperate search for personal fulfillment. On my iPod, I listen to Third Eye Blind's "Semi-Charmed Life." This popular song from the nineties captures the emptiness of a partying lifestyle that never satisfies. Expressed with an almost youthful naiveté, Third Eye Blind confesses, "I want something else, to get me through this semi-charmed kind of life."

But if I leap off of my lofty perch and candidly look at myself and other believers around me, I wonder how much better off we are than the rest of the world. Author Tony Campolo points out, "Most Christians I know have just enough of the Gospel to make them miserable, but not enough to make them joyful." I agree. All too often, we seem to be following the same cycle of thirsting, seeking, and settling. As much as we believe in our head that Christ transforms us into a new creation, something seems lacking in our heart. We hear sermons on Sunday exhorting us to live an abundant Christian life, but come Monday morning, we find ourselves living a "semi-charmed kind of life." In the end, a happy, joy-filled life becomes something that we think of as a future gig, attainable only in eternity.

Yet when I open up my Bible, I never find the Christian life described as anything half-baked. Christ doesn't talk much about happiness, but I see the promise of joy repeated constantly throughout the New Testament. Jesus tells his followers that when we follow him, our joy will be "complete" (John 15:11). He even tells us that we'll "leap for joy" (Luke 6:23). Paul explains that the Holy Spirit will produce a lasting joy inside of us (Gal. 5:22–23), making it a key trait of our faith. That's why he can confidently tell the Philippians to "be joyful always" (Phil. 4:4, NIV) and the Thessalonian church to "rejoice always" (1 Thess. 5:16). Peter has his say as well, pointing out that when we believe in Christ, we are filled with "an inexpressible and glorious joy" (1 Peter 1:8).

But if Jesus and the apostles are correct, why are so many believers struggling with something I call a "joy gap"—a separation between the promises of Scripture and the very real letdown they experience in their daily lives? I can see only two explanations. Either the Bible hypes joy and offers us an unrealistic portrait of its practical impact, or we are somehow missing out, leaving God's precious gift unclaimed.

I am convinced that the source of this "joy gap" rests firmly on our shoulders. Simply put, we are confused by joy. We fail to grasp what joy really is, how it differs from happiness, what it is not, and how it can be fully experienced in our lives. In fact, I've come to look at joy being spoken of in Christian circles in the same way that the word *inconceivable* is used for comic effect in *The Princess Bride*. In the film, Vizzini is a loveable but clueless villain who has a habit of responding with "inconceivable" each time the unlikely occurs. After several repeated occasions, his cohort Inigo Montoya finally turns to Vizzini and says, "You keep using that word. I do not think it means what you think it means." In the same way, maybe we in the church need to take a lesson from Inigo Montoya. Perhaps the way we are using the word *joy* is different from what it actually means in Scripture.

Not that we are alone in our confusion. The history of God's people is littered with semi-charmed lives. The newly freed Israelites wandering in the desert witnessed God's power daily, but their constant complaining caused a massive exodus of joy from their camp. The generations that followed had their share of mountaintop experiences, but they lost joy bit by bit in chronic disobedience and disbelief. King Solomon, one of ancient Israel's greatest kings, is a case study of the joy gap in action. Solomon possessed unmatched wisdom and wealth throughout the world; more than anyone else, he should have been the poster child for a joy-filled life. Yet Solomon's blessings only brought him confusion over what could offer lasting joy, peace, and meaning. His final writing, the book of Ecclesiastes, reveals his true spiritual state: it is the most depressing, joy-starved entry in the entire Bible.

Over the centuries, Christians haven't fared much better than Solomon and the Israelites. Many of the New Testament letters were written to correct bad teaching that was robbing the early church of joy. "What has happened to your joy?" Paul in effect asks the Galatians. The medieval church was even worse: bad doctrine and rigid legalism burned joy at the stake. Even a Protestant hero like Martin Luther missed the mark. Evangelicals may love his doctrine, but when you peek into his personal life, you quickly realize that joy wasn't a quality he naturally exhibited.

A Stacked Deck

As I look at the state of the church today, I am afraid we are not any better off than our spiritual forefathers were. In fact, I am sometimes tempted to raise the white flag, convinced that the deck is stacked against gaining a true understanding of this gift. Joy is such a difficult concept to characterize, after all. Defining it is much like trying to hold Jell-O in your hands. When we try to explain what joy means, it ends up slipping out the sides looking like something else—usually happiness, peace, or gladness. But biblical joy is clearly distinct from each of these words.

In his book *Megatrends*, John Naisbitt identifies a trend he calls "high tech/high touch." Interestingly, his ideas offer some insight into the joy gap. Naisbitt argues that the success of a technology has as much to do with the human element—how comfortable people are with the product—as it does with its innovation. In other words, as revolutionary as a technology may be, the marketplace will only adopt it if consumers easily understand what the technology is and how it can benefit them. When I apply Naisbitt's ideas to joy, I think joy struggles with the *high touch* test. People don't intuitively understand how it is different from "being happy" or "feeling good."

Joy's identity problems are even more apparent when contrasted with grace. Visual images flashing through my mind easily convey the essence of grace to me. Jesus dying on the cross in the Gospels. The bishop pardoning a guilty Jean Valjean in *Les Misérables*. A choir bellowing out the sweet words of "Amazing Grace." If grace has the solid texture of "meat and potatoes," joy comes off as having the airy texture of cotton candy—hard to grasp and a struggle to take hold of.

Culture certainly adds to the confusion. On his fiftieth birthday, music legend Bob Dylan was interviewed by *Rolling Stone* magazine. When asked whether he was happy, Dylan responded, "Those are yuppie words, happiness and unhappiness. It's not happiness or unhappiness, it's blessed or unblessed." This brief interchange between Dylan and the interviewer illustrates the dominant view of what constitutes a well-lived life. To most people, happiness is the key motivator. It's what drives them to work each morning. It's what keeps them company at night. People measure happiness in "yuppie" terms—career, wealth, toys, convenient relationships, and mountaintop experiences.

In this context, joy is simply treated as just another word for happiness. You see this all around in popular culture. MasterCard proclaims "Life takes joy ... Life takes MasterCard." M&M Mars wants to satisfy your cravings with an Almond Joy. At night, after your candy bar snack, you can crawl into bed with a copy of *The Joy of Sex*. Yet when joy becomes just another term to express pleasure or delight, it ceases to be the same concept used in the Scriptures. Instead of being a permanent trait of our Christ-filled life, joy becomes something much more superficial—a reflection of our mood or emotional state.

When I look around at how joy is talked about in the Christian community, I mutter to myself: *Et tu, Brute?* Joy is often reduced to being a mere by-product of Christian behavior. Browse around your local Christian bookstore and you will see evidence of this reality all over the shelves. *The Joy of Serving. The Joy of Prayer. The Joy of Financial Freedom.* In fact, a quick search on Christianbook.com shows over seventy titles containing *The Joy of* _____ in them. These may be worthwhile books, but notice how the nature of joy becomes muddied. Joy ends up sounding like a fringe benefit we receive when we behave in a certain way or perform a given activity.

To top it off, our postmodern society is paced for happiness, not joy. We live in a "real time" world of instant stock quotes, BlackBerry devices, and 24/7 news streamed to cell phones. Living in this environment, our spiritual life will often beg to follow suit—even when we don't realize it. Our faith can become preoccupied with immediacy and dependent on "on demand" results. Consequently, joy usually comes and goes in proportion to the "real time" state of our lives. When things are good, we radiate joy to everyone around us. But when times get rough, our shoulders slump in defeat and discouragement.

Pidgin Joy

"Pidgin English" was a term commonly used by nineteenth-century British traders to describe the simplified or broken version of the English language that the Chinese spoke in ports. Instead of learning the full English vocabulary, Chinese routinely injected native Cantonese words and pronunciations in their English phrases. The word *pidgin*, in fact, is believed to be a Chinese mispronunciation of the word *business*.

As a writer, I love to play with words. I'll tweak a sentence over and over again in an effort to convey the precise meaning that I intend. So when I mulled over how to best express our confusion over joy, I found *pidgin* leaping off of the page. More than any other expression I've come across, it seems to convey most accurately the underlying problem we have with biblical joy. We get a taste of it, but rather than fully embrace God's gift, we mix in our own rough and ready ideas. The end result is pidgin joy, a broken and lesser version of the real thing.

If you believe the Scriptures, joy is far more than a thesaurus entry for happiness or a by-product of Christian behavior. While grace is God's priceless gift to the unsaved, joy is his most tangible and transformative gift that he gives to his followers this side of heaven. Joy is dynamic proof of our future hope as believers and our greatest distinguisher to a cynical world held hostage by life's circumstances. G. K. Chesterton adds, "Joy ... is the gigantic secret of the Christian."

I am writing this book, not because I am an expert on the subject, but because I want to fully discover the joy that is so clearly promised to us as believers.

My search for joy began about a decade ago. At the time, I was living a semi-charmed life; the thirst, seek, and settle train that I was on nearly ruined me. I was in my late twenties and experiencing a "quarter life crisis." With the second hand of my life's clock ticking away in my ear, I grew dissatisfied. I was craving something more.

My whole life up to that point had been steeped in "All Things Christian." As the son of a pastor, I'd grown up in the church and made a decision for Christ at the age of nine. I graduated from a Christian college. I married a strong believer, and we had three Christians-in-training growing up in our home. Throughout my life, I had read about joy in the Bible and heard it proclaimed by my pastor. Yet I never experienced the kind of joy that was promised, and I slowly became disillusioned. It seemed natural, then, to look for joy in the world around me.

CHAPTER 2

NOTHING BUT A YUPPIE WORD

Anyone who says money can't buy happiness
doesn't know where to shop.
—Lovey Howell, *Gilligan's Island*

The purpose of life is to be happy.
—Dalai Lama

Joy … happiness … whatever.

I didn't care what you called it, I just wanted something. Anything. I was tired of "walking the line" as I always had done before. The straight and narrow path had turned joyless and was starting to suffocate me. I began to sound like the French revolutionary Saint-Juste exclaiming during the height of the French Revolution, "We don't want happiness in the next world. We want it next Monday!"

My career emerged as my ticket out of the rut I was in. I had struggled during my first few years out of college with entry-level jobs. But I had just landed a new senior-level role that was finally going to take me somewhere. For the first time, the world valued me, and I responded by embracing it with both arms open wide. The happiness and fulfillment at my doorstep seemed much more tangible than the Christian joy that seemed to be ever dangled before me like a carrot on a stick.

In defining happiness, *Webster's Dictionary* effectively sums up what I wanted out of life at the time: "a state of well-being and contentment." I wanted to be a success. Earn a nice salary. Drive a nice car. Perhaps even make a name for myself.

Don't Worry, Be Happy

The pursuit of happiness, it seems to me, has become the *zeitgeist* of the postmodern world. *Zeitgeist*, meaning "spirit of the age," describes the general outlook or feeling of a particular time in history. "Billions of people walking around like Happy Meals with legs" was how one teenage television show characterized our Western culture. This description is certainly jaded, but I am haunted by the grain of truth that can be found in it. After all, consider the ways in which we spend our time and money nowadays; much is focused on being happy.

The corporate world certainly realizes this truth. "Sex sells" is the old marketing adage. But the reality is that personal happiness is the key motivator for *every* advertising campaign, from cars to colas, from investments to impotency drugs.

This happiness trend goes beyond clever marketing, however. It extends into media and policymaking circles as well. The BBC devoted prime airtime to a popular six-part series called *The Happiness Formula*, exploring different perspectives on what makes people happy. I've read that social scientists are touting a new measuring stick for nations called Gross

National Happiness. To assess the country's quality of life, the British government has started to tout the concept of a happiness index. Spotting the obvious trend, a British sociologist quipped, "It seems that the ditty 'if you're happy and you know it, clap your hands' is about to become the principal slogan in British public life."

As I pursued happiness with reckless abandon, I had few distractions to hinder me. This has not always been the case. When our great-grandparents grew up, for example, they were far more concerned with their very survival than we ever are today. They had to contend with world wars, an economic depression, and political revolutions. Not so anymore. In fact, our entire contemporary society seems to be oriented toward being happy.

"You Deserve It"

The average American makes far more money today than ever before. Just a few generations ago, a man would work long hours in polluted factories or toil in fields under the hot sun to make sure a family's basic needs were met. Disposable income was a luxury that only a handful of people possessed. All this has changed, especially with the high percentage of double-income families today. Luxury, if you watch commercials on television, has become a middle-class word.

Even when extra cash dries up, businesses are eager to help people like me out. Instead of purchasing a used Honda Accord, I can lease a brand new BMW for the same monthly payment. Rather than buy a small portable TV that fits my current budget, I can purchase a new flat-screen, high definition television today on credit and pay nothing until next year.

"Play Hard"

The idea of a five-day work week, annual summer vacations, and paid holidays are so ingrained in our contemporary culture that they seem more like rights than privileges. With more free time and extra cash, we participate more and more in entertaining ourselves: going to movies, watching around-the-clock football on Sundays, or vacationing at a summer cottage on the lake.

"Ask Your Doctor Today"

Medical advances over the past century have eradicated many diseases, found ways to cope with others, and allowed people to control both physical and mental illnesses and pain through medication. You can hardly find an hour of prime time television go by without a pharmaceutical company promoting their latest anti-depression or impotency drug. "Fix your problem and you'll be happy" is the subliminal message.

"To Each His Own"

As long as we don't break the law, we can generally do most anything that we want to do. In fact, I can't think of any societal pressures or cultural handcuffs that dissuade personal behavior. Homosexuality is a right. Abortion is a choice. Divorce is the norm. When a lifestyle change becomes a means to a happier life, then society nods its head in approval. "Not that there's anything wrong with it," goes the classic *Seinfeld* line. Personal fulfillment thus becomes the driving force and bottom line behind ethics.

"Make Love, Not War"

At least from the perspective of North America and Europe, the world is largely at peace. Yes, there have been two wars in Iraq, Middle East tensions, and periodic terrorist activity over the past two decades, but these wars and attacks have only directly affected a small percentage of the population. As a result, we don't spend much time thinking about our physical survival. Long life seems like a given.

I was watching the television show *24* a couple years back. In one particular tension-packed episode, George Mason, one of the show's main characters, discovers that he has been contaminated with radiation fallout. The doctors give him just twenty-four hours before he will die of poisoning. George has an estranged relationship with his son, so he immediately tries to reconcile with him. He then recalls the lost opportunities in his life, reflecting on what could have been.

I have a suspicion that most screenplay writers of these kinds of shows have a secret desire to land a dramatic quote that transcends the storyline and hits home with viewers—a nugget of truth that is discussed around the water cooler the next morning and gets posted on the Internet Movie Database. Perhaps that was the motivation behind George's final piece of advice to a colleague when he said his goodbyes: "Find something that makes you happy, and do it. Because everything else is all just background noise." George's dying words, as penned by a Hollywood screenwriter, were probably intended as profound words to live by. Yet in doing so, the screenwriter unintentionally summed up the paper-thin spirit of our age: *happiness is what life is all about.*

The Pursuit

We may be more preoccupied with being happy today than any other generation in history, but the pursuit of happiness is nothing new. You would surely have to go back to the Garden of Eden to find its starting point. Philosopher William James believed happiness is the "secret motive" inside the heart of every man. And while the world may always be on a constant lookout for the happy life, no one has ever been able to agree on how you can actually attain it.

Historically, happiness has been associated with good fortune or favorable circumstances. Perhaps it is not surprising, then, that every Germanic word for "happiness" originates from a common root word meaning "luck."

The Greek philosopher Aristotle and his contemporaries, however, despised the idea that good luck dictated how happy a person could be. He argued that a person can be happy even when he can't control or predict what is going to happen to him. Happiness was attained by pursuing virtue; it was the reward of a well-lived life. This classical perspective was revived during the Enlightenment and was widely held among America's Founding Fathers. Ben Franklin put it like this: "Virtue and happiness are mother and daughter." In fact, this line of thinking is clearly seen in the most famous line of the U.S. Declaration of Independence: "We hold these truths to be self-evident, that all men ... are endowed by their Creator with certain unalienable Rights, that among these are Life, Liberty and *the pursuit of Happiness*" (italics added).

In contrast, most medical scientists hold no such lofty or philosophical notions. They contend that happiness is not determined by luck, circumstances, or virtue at all. Instead, the primary source of happiness is found in a person's gene pool. Some people are simply hardwired to be happy, scientists suggest, while some are not.

Buddhists, on the other hand, believe that a person's happiness is based on their spiritual nature. According to the Dalai Lama, the purpose of life is to be happy. This state of happiness is achieved by making one's inner self right through meditation. Through this process, a person is able to let go of his or her desires and get away from the self-centeredness that causes unhappiness and discontent.

By and large, however, I believe most of us frankly don't care what the ancients, scientists, or Buddhists think. We seek happiness by following two basic rules. First, eliminate all of the bad stuff from your life that you can—things like depression, bad relationships, poor health, and inconvenient obligations. Second, fill your life with good stuff—a challenging career, exciting relationships, plenty of goodies, and cool experiences.

When people begin to seek this kind of good life, they usually take one of two paths. First, the pursuit of happiness often turns into a quest for the Next Big Thing. I convince myself that whatever is new is going to fulfill my desires. An iPod, a fall outfit from the Gap, or a new car. An episode of the television show *Ally McBeal* aired in 1997 drove home this popular view of happiness: "At some point we have to face the certain reality: despite all the good the world seems to offer, true happiness can only be found in one thing—shopping."

Other people, however, don't get a buzz from going to the mall or buying a new gadget. Instead, they look for happiness through cool mountaintop experiences. An exciting career for some. World travel or extreme sports for others. A few seek to make the world a better place through volunteerism. Happiness is gained by stringing together as many of these interesting and meaningful encounters as you can.

Expiration Dates

I was not a very good rebel. I tried to run from God's Word, but I never stopped believing it. After a few months of pursuing happiness my own way, my heart just wasn't into it anymore. I may have not experienced the joy I desired following Christ, but abandoning him was proving even worse. I was miserable. Inevitably, I had a "prodigal moment," the sort of instant awakening that the younger son in Jesus' parable must have experienced when he was down on his hands and knees in a pigpen. So, before I ruined my life, I returned to my heavenly Father. Oh, I still wanted to pursue happiness alright, but I knew I couldn't experience it apart from my faith.

With God now in tow, I resumed my career pursuits with a new energy and passion. I began chasing the coattails of the Silicon Valley dream. I invented an internet software program that received enthusiastic responses by users, great press clippings, and at least some attention from the big internet names of the day. I decided that the small East Coast company I worked for could never do much with my product, so I looked for a suitor in Silicon Valley.

I did it. No, I was not one of the strike-it-rich dot-com millionaires who made headlines in the mid-nineties, but I followed shortly after them. My software invention was acquired by NetObjects, a promising start-up in the heart of Silicon Valley. Feeling the Lord's direction and blessing, I moved my family out west with visions of a modern-day gold rush dancing in my head. While the product itself wasn't important enough to garner much money, it did get a brief mention on CNN and a blurb in the *Wall Street Journal*. The whole experience seemed very significant, to me anyway.

Once there, my career was on a nonstop path straight to the top. Every several months, I'd get a promotion, moving from engineer, to manager, to director, to senior director, and to vice president within a mere two years. Although my company's initial public offering was not wildly successful like so many other dot coms of the time, we appeared to be poised for a steady upward path to the stratosphere. Success was not just at the office either; my personal life was finally reaping the same fruit. I was growing in my Christian walk, involved in budding church ministries, and giving more priority to my marriage and family than ever before. Surely I was living the prototype for the joy-filled Christian life.

A Magic That Fades

During this past year, my family took a vacation to Walt Disney World, the self-proclaimed Happiest Place on Earth. From dawn till dusk, we spent five days experiencing the wonders, thrills, and excitement of the Magic Kingdom and the other Disney theme parks. We had an incredible experience. But after a week there, even my three boys were exhausted and ready to head home.

Of all the attractions, my favorite was an interactive 3-D movie entitled Mickey's PhilharMagic. In a specially designed theater, Disney ingeniously combines state-of-the-art 3-D photography on a giant screen with in-theater effects, such as water sprinkles, food aromas, and wind. The result is nothing less than spectacular. We found ourselves going into this attraction every time we passed it. So, on our final day at the park, we decided to go one last time. This time around, however, the newness had started to wear off. The magic had begun to fade. In the end, I realized that even Disney Imagineering can't sustain happiness longer than a few days.

Disney World has historically been viewed as a coveted employer for college students and twentysomethings. After all, if a student is working his or her way through college, why not do so in the Happiest Place on Earth? Yet studies show that employee satisfaction at Disney is no different than anywhere else. Disney employees are happy when the pay is good and career paths exist. But when these factors are lacking, then employee turnover rises.

In a grand irony, the Happiest Place on Earth offers perhaps the most compelling evidence of the inevitable shortcomings of happiness. Happiness, no matter how it is attained, has an expiration date.

Luck, virtue, genes, meditation, shopping, experiences, and Mickey Mouse ears. Each is said to offer happiness. But the real issue is not so much what to do to *be* happy. Instead, it is our inability to *stay* happy. For no matter how we get into a state of fulfillment and contentment, we just can't stay there.

Why am I even surprised? The pleasure I receive over a fatter paycheck, new house, or new convertible always becomes less exciting in a shorter amount of time than I ever think it will. I just can't seem to accept the fact that anytime I experience something new, I quickly adapt to it, and it then becomes my definition of "normal." Once it becomes ordinary, however, I lose the happiness I received in pursuing the thing in the first place. Continuing the cycle, I then start looking for the Next Big Thing to pursue.

A Ship That Sinks

While at NetObjects, I was on a mountaintop. For a moment in time, I felt like Leonardo DiCaprio perched on the bow of the *Titanic* shouting, "I'm king of the world!" But not long after that, the ship I was on hit an iceberg. The bottom dropped out of the internet boom and dot com stocks began to tumble; NetObjects was one of those that was hit hard. Sensing that God was closing this chapter of my life, I gave up on Silicon Valley. I left my dream job and moved back east. In a whirlwind of months, I found myself going from the prospect of being a successful millionaire to just being glad I had a job to pay the bills. To make matters worse, the position I found myself in when I moved back to Massachusetts was a major letdown. I stayed at the company because I believed it was God's leading, but nearly every day I struggled to be motivated. With a chill running down my back, I asked myself: was I destined for a semi-charmed life once again?

In my search for joy over a six-year span, I ran away from God for a season. I returned to him and lived an exemplary life. I bought into the Next Big Thing, and I reached several mountaintops in my career. But no matter what I did, the end result was the same. The happiness I was chasing in the world didn't last.

Happiness offered a glimpse of the joy I was so thirsty for, but it left me feeling unsatisfied. "Happiness in this world, when it comes, comes incidentally," said author Nathaniel Hawthorne. "Make it the object of pursuit, and it leads us on a wild-goose chase, and is never attained." Real joy, I discovered, lay some-where else.

CHAPTER 3

FLICKERS OF A FAR-OFF COUNTRY

All joy (as distinct from mere pleasure, still more amusement)
emphasizes our pilgrim status; always reminds, beckons, awakens desire.
Our best havings are wantings.
—C. S. Lewis

To see a world in a grain of sand
And heaven in a wild flower,
Hold infinity in the palm of your hand
And eternity in an hour.
—William Blake

"Pinch me, I must be dreaming," I told my wife, Kimberly, as I woke up on a snowy February morning in Breckinridge, Colorado. How often do you get a chance to spend a day skiing with one of your all-time heroes?

A year had passed since I left the high-tech world behind. Convinced of God's calling, I was now making a go of it as a full-time Christian author. My earlier concern about getting stuck in a humdrum existence now seemed comical, given the uncertain nature of trying to make a living by writing. Risky yes, boring no.

I was in the Rocky Mountain state to meet with a respected Christian thinker, someone I'd looked up to for years. In an email exchange months before, he told me to look him up if I was ever in the Colorado area. Once my family decided to go on a ski vacation later that year, we began to arrange a time to get together. Being an avid skier himself, he invited me to spend a day with him at Vail.

I had skied at many of the Colorado resorts, but never there. I had heard from friends, however, of how spectacular Vail's legendary Back Bowls were. Containing thousands of acres of massive, bowl-like mountain runs, the Back Bowls are considered some of the best skiing terrain on the planet.

The two of us met up that morning, and we made our way up the mountain. Considering the company I was with, I was far more preoccupied with the conversation than the mountain we were skiing on. The fact that we were at Vail seemed inconsequential.

As we talked, we made our way from the front of the mountain to the Back Bowls. But when I got off of the ski lift and glided over to the top of the run, my world came to a sudden stop.

The panoramic view I was looking at left me speechless. The rugged, snowcapped peaks of the Continental Divide formed a majestic backdrop to the seven powdery snow bowls right before me. Everything around me, to borrow from Psalm 65, was clothed with joy. The thrill of skiing with my hero, as great as that was, now seemed trivial by comparison. The excitement of a technical descent down a double black diamond run also seemed ho-hum. All that fluttered through my mind was that I had just caught a glimpse of heaven. I was overjoyed and wanted more.

Common Joy

Inside every great work of art is a piece of the artist himself, a fingerprint that the master permanently leaves behind on his creation. Pick any Shakespeare tragedy; its brilliant prose will never be confused with another author's work. A Rembrandt portrait cannot help but stand out among a gallery of lesser paintings. So too in the age of movies, an M. Night Shyamalan film like *Signs* or *Sixth Sense* has a distinct style from other thrillers you'll find playing at your local multiplex.

In much the same way, God leaves his fingerprints all over creation. The whole universe, in fact, screams of his creative genius. Just a quick trip to the Colorado Rockies or Niagara Falls can convince even a skeptic of God's power and might. However, I am coming to realize that God does more than just demonstrate his awesome strength in the world; he also reveals his joy.

"Shout for joy to God, all the earth," says the psalmist in Psalm 66. He continues in later psalms. "Let all the trees of the forest sing for joy," goes Psalm 96. Psalm 98 adds, "Let the rivers clap their hands, let the mountains sing together for joy." The psalmist is obviously using anthropomorphism in these passages for poetic purposes. However, I wonder if he is alluding to a deeper truth as well—the idea that God's creation does, in a real way, display the joy of the Lord.

Most of the things I come in contact with on a daily basis are ordinary and commonplace. Concrete, computers, and coconuts, for instance, are strictly earthly stuff. We make or grow, and use or consume them. They're around for awhile, but they never last. The happiness and pleasure that we encounter in our lives falls into this category. I can take a cool swim on a sultry summer day, eat a warm slice of blueberry pie, and witness a dog licking the face of my son. Each of these simple delights touches my senses or tickles my emotions for the brief moments in which I experience them. But once they are done, I rarely think about them further.

Not everything this world has to offer is so commonplace, however. There are things that I can experience that mysteriously go beyond "normal life." A great work of music, art, or literature. A powerful worship service. Or a majestic mountain landscape. In an unexplainable way, these experiences take me beyond my ordinary world and give me a taste of the eternal. They give me joy. "There is not one blade of grass," said the Protestant reformer John Calvin, "there is no color in this world that is not intended to make us rejoice." The French poet Paul Claudel had a similar reaction when he first listened to Beethoven's *Fifth Symphony*, remarking, "Now I know that at the heart of the universe there is joy."

Theologians use a concept called "common grace" to refer to the undeserved blessings given by God to all humankind. God's role in creation, the restraint of evil, and the gift of a person's conscience are typical examples. Common grace is distinct from "special grace" or "saving grace," which is offered through Jesus Christ only for those who believe in him.

In a remarkable way, joy closely parallels grace in how it is expressed in the world. The type of joy that is talked about in the Scriptures is that "special joy" that resides exclusively in the heart of a Christian. However, there is another type of joy in the universe, something that I call "common joy."

Every man and woman is created *imago Dei* — "in the image of God" — the God of joy. As part of his design, he implanted something inside of us that produces a deep spiritual longing for the eternal. Paul indicates as much in Acts 14:17: "Yet he has not left himself without testimony: He ... fills your hearts with joy." I sense this when I listen to a Vivaldi symphony or read a Gerard Manley Hopkins poem. And I certainly experienced this yearning on that day in Vail, Colorado.

Common joy produces a hunger that we cannot satisfy. Our earthly bodies are somehow ill-equipped to handle this nectar of heaven. We can taste the joy, but not drink it; we can catch a glimpse, but it remains just out of our reach. "Joy flickers on the razor-edge of the present and is gone," reflects C. S. Lewis in an early poem. Yet despite the fact that this longing remains unfulfilled in our lives, it can be more splendid than any happiness or pleasure we can experience. Lewis says in *The Pilgrim's Regress*, "This hunger is better than any other fullness; this poverty better than all other wealth."

When the eternal touches our world, joy is the inevitable result. We see it in the sanctified life of a believer — he or she experiences joy from the everlasting God living inside. However, through conduits like art and nature, we can also discover common joy in the world itself. Pope John Paul II once spoke of the joy that is found in the work of creative artists:

> Authentic and humble artists are perfectly well aware, no matter what kind of beauty characterizes their handiwork, that their paintings, sculptures or creations are nothing else but the reflection of God's Beauty. No matter how strong the charm of their music and words, they know that their works are only a distant echo of God's Word.

When we experience joy in this way, God seems to be hinting at something greater. It's a flicker of a far-off country. Consider two vignettes that illustrate the power of God's common joy that he reveals through creation.

That Old Ache

The film *The Shawshank Redemption* chronicles Andy Dufresne, a thirty-year-old banker who is sentenced to life in prison after being wrongfully convicted of committing a double murder. His new incarcerated life consists of colorless clothes, tasteless food, menial jobs, abuse by other prisoners, and a home of cement and granite. However, during one scene of the film, joy rains down on Shawshank prison in the form of music. In so doing, it offers Andy and his fellow prisoners a sense of the eternal that they are desperately missing from their lives.

One afternoon, several years after arriving at Shawshank, Andy is busy performing bookkeeping and accounting duties inside the prison warden's office. A delivery arrives for the prison library. Books, stacks of old records, and a record player are among the goods sent by the state. As Andy thumbs through the records in the boxes, he finds an opera LP. Seeing that the guards are busy elsewhere, Andy places the record on the record player and begins to play a song. Heavenly soprano voices soon pierce the silence of the warden's office.

Andy is moved by the music, and after several moments of listening by himself, he is no longer able to control his enthusiasm—he simply *must* share this music with everyone else. In spite of the severe punishment that he knows will follow, Andy locks the office doors, turns on the public address system, and holds the microphone next to the speaker. A short squeal from the speakers gets everyone's attention, after which the opera music begins playing throughout the whole prison. From the infirmary to the recreational courtyard to the laundry facility, every prisoner instantly stops what he is doing, looks up to the sky, and simply listens. Reflecting on the impact that the music had on the inmates, Andy's friend recalls:

> I have no idea to this day what those two Italian ladies were singing about. Truth is, I don't want to know. Some things are best left unsaid. I like to think they were singing about something so beautiful it can't be expressed in words and makes your heart ache because of it. I tell you, those voices soared, higher and farther than anybody in a gray place dares to dream. It was like some beautiful bird flapped into our drab little cage and made those walls dissolve away. And for the briefest of moments, every last man in Shawshank felt free.

The music reverberates the message that life really exists beyond the walls of the prison. The inmates are awakened from their slumber of despair and meaninglessness, even if but for a moment. To the man, each Shawshank prisoner experiences joy.

Yearning for the Eternal

Until the 1990s, Henryk Górecki was an obscure Polish composer whom only a handful of people in the classical music community had even heard of. However, in 1992, the London Symphony recorded his Symphony no. 3, called *Symphony of Sorrowful Songs*. Soon after, it became the most unexpected musical phenomenon of the decade. The recording rose not only on the classical charts of *Billboard* magazine, but climbed to number 7 on the popular charts as well. Incredibly, the album went to sell more than one million copies.

Since that time, many have speculated on the reason for the "Górecki Phenomenon," as it has come to be known. Most explanations focus squarely on the unique rhythmic qualities of his music. But when I listen to Górecki, I know exactly the reason for its popularity: the joy a person experiences while listening to it. Górecki's Symphony no. 3 produces what C. S. Lewis called "that old ache" inside of its listeners—an unexplainable yearning for the eternal. Even some inside the classical music community seem to have picked up on this. One critic describes Górecki's "sense of transcendental awe" that flows from his music. Another music writer adds, "Górecki's music ... [contrasts] the holy with the mundane, the everyday with the eternal, or ... the sacred with the profane ... Górecki is able to connect with our innermost humanity through the experience of time he creates in his music."

In the 1990s' musical scene of hip-hop and grunge, a classical song was able to go beyond public radio into the mainstream because it offered listeners something else—a taste of joy. Or as Charles Colson concludes, Górecki "shows us the incredible power of music to reach into the soul of a jaded world. And through Górecki's music, Christ teaches us to sing."

Dumb Idols

Common grace helps point humankind toward Christ's saving grace. Likewise, common joy is meant to give us a taste of something greater, something that transcends the practical, the concrete, and the temporal. The danger we face is becoming so preoccupied with the thing that gives us the joy that we forget all about the source of that longing—Jesus Christ himself.

I am a sucker for great films, and I can easily become fixated by them. Something is triggered inside of me, spurring me to watch them again and again and again. I experience joy when I watch Ray Kinsella pursue his crazy dream in *Field of Dreams*. I feel God's eternal hope when I watch Andy and Red reach Mexico in *The Shawshank Redemption*. The understated romance of Darcy and Elizabeth in *Pride and Prejudice* becomes an ideal for how romantic love should be. But just like anything else in the world, when I let these things take over my life, I turn them into idols. In the essay *The Weight of Glory*, C. S. Lewis explains:

> The books or the music in which we thought the beauty was located will betray us if we trust in them; it was not in them, it only came through them, and what came through them was longing. These things—the beauty, the memory of our own past—are good images of what we really desire; but if they are mistaken for the thing itself they turn into dumb idols, breaking the hearts of their worshippers. For they are not the thing itself; they are only the scent of a flower we have not found, the echo of a tune we have not heard, news from a country we have not visited.

There's a second problem with focusing too much on the conduits of joy. Just like earthly happiness, the yearning never lasts. If I return to Vail's Back Bowls some day, I will still appreciate the view, but I probably won't have another "heaven sighting." Similarly, I've seen *Field of Dreams* one too many times already to ever recapture that same joyous feeling I once had when I watched it.

The Serious Business of Heaven

I had been thirsty my entire life. In my search for the real thing, I discovered common joy. I sensed immediately that I had found something deeply spiritual and God-breathed; it was far more authentic than the happiness I looked for in the world and the pidgin-joy ideas of my past. But at the same time, I quickly found out that you can't live with it. Common joy changes moments of time, but not your entire life. There had to be more to real joy than this, I convinced myself. C. S. Lewis wrote boldly in an essay that "joy is the serious business of Heaven." That's the kind of joy I was after.

The world couldn't deliver the goods. Art, music, and nature couldn't either. I became convinced that if I was ever going to experience a joy-filled life, then I had to revisit where I had begun my search in the first place.

PART 2

CONSIDER IT JOY

CHAPTER 4

A BLESSED INVASION

The joy of Jesus is a miracle,
it is not the outcome of my doing things or of my being good,
but of my receiving the very nature of God.
—Oswald Chambers

I have told you this so that my joy may be in you
and that your joy may be complete.
—John 15:11

A Coke bottle drops from the sky. That's the surprising intro-duction to modern society that a bushman gets as he walks through the Kalahari Desert in the 1980 screwball comedy *The Gods Must Be Crazy.* In the film, the bushman isn't sure what to make of a bottle falling from a passing airplane, and so he concludes that it must be a gift from the gods. After he takes it back to his tribe, together they try to figure out what to do with it. A musical instrument. A fire starter. Perhaps a cooking utensil. But in the end, they give up. Thinking the gift is more trouble than it is worth, the bushman goes on a journey across the desert to return the bottle to the gods.

All my life, I viewed joy as something like that Coke bottle. It descended unexpectedly from the heavens and fell into my world. And like the bushman, I had been puzzled my whole life about what to make of the gift. I tried various ways to mold it into something I could understand and work with. But when my dumbed-down versions of joy let me down, the whole experience became disillusioning. In my mind, God must be crazy for making the kind of promises that he does.

I became determined to shed my pidgin understanding of joy once and for all. Over the years, I'd studied various passages in the Bible that deal with joy. I probably even led a Bible study or two on the subject. But I wanted to look again at the Scriptures in light of joy and see what I had always been missing.

It's no exaggeration to say that joy, in all its many forms, is a driving force of Scripture, being sprinkled over 350 times from Genesis through Revelation. It sweeps through the Garden of Eden, the Promised Land, Jesus' earthly ministry, the early church, and the future second coming of Christ. "Joy is the great note all through the Bible," seconds Oswald Chambers.

There are several Hebrew and Greek words used in the Scriptures that express *joy* and its derivatives, such as *to rejoice* and *joyful.* But if I summarize these various terms, I can translate joy as an "extreme delight or gladness that is outwardly expressed." A translator may be pleased with this definition, but I wasn't. To me, it sounded far too much like the happiness that always produced a dead end in my life.

I became convinced that there was more to the story than textual analysis alone. As I read through more of the Scriptures, it dawned on me that even in spots of the Bible that do not explicitly talk about joy, there is a clear undercurrent of joy throughout the text. I realized that if I was going to fully understand joy, then the underlying motivations of God throughout the Old and New Testaments must also be considered.

Plainly speaking, the God who is revealed in the pages of the Bible is a God of joy. He's a loving Father, bursting at the seams, so to speak, in his desire to share his delight with the people he created. "He will rejoice over you with singing," exclaims Zephaniah (Zeph. 3:17). Charles Spurgeon adds, "Man was not originally made to mourn; he was made to rejoice." Jesus Christ emphasizes this truth in John 15. After calling his followers to obedience and remaining steadfast, he concludes, "I have told you this so that my joy may be in you and that your joy may be complete" (v. 11). Joy emerges from Scripture as one of the primary ways in which God chooses to reveal himself, to express his amazing love to humankind, and to equip us for living in a fallen world.

Like a bolt of lightning from above, the nature of joy finally hit me, and I discovered a meaty biblical response to the pidgin joy that plagued me. Joy is something worlds apart from an emotional reaction or a smiley face. Instead, *joy is nothing less than the nature of God pumped through our bloodstream.* It's a blessed invasion of the Spirit of God deep into my soul. Oswald Chambers puts it like this: "Jesus does not come to a man and say 'Cheer up,' he plants within a man the miracle of the joy of God's own nature."

I know, defining joy in this way sounds a bit mysterious. After all, there is hardly anything more mystifying in the life of a Christian than trying to grasp the indwelling of the Holy Spirit. While the particulars of what goes on inside of us may be difficult or impossible to grasp, don't take this definition as sounding too abstract to make any practical significance for your life.

I am convinced that if we can just grab hold of the fact that joy is *really* the nature of God living inside of us, then our Christian walk will never be the same. Our confusion and disillusionment will start to fade away, and the "joy gap"—the crack between God's promises of joy and our actual experience in the real world—will begin to vanish.

The Six Dimensions of Biblical Joy

Stereograms are three-dimensional images hidden within another picture. They became popular several years ago with the rise of computerized art. On first glance, a picture with a stereogram doesn't look like anything out of the ordinary. But if you stare long enough, the 3-D images buried within the picture start to jump out at you. The divine nature of joy is much like a stereogram. I can look superficially at joy, and it comes across as little more than ordinary happiness. But when I embrace the idea that my joy comes straight from the God living inside of me, then several realities of joy start to jump out.

A Permanent Presence

Joy in Scripture is associated with the presence of God. However, in the Old Testament, joy has a more episodic quality to it, something we experience during worship, celebrations, or intimate moments with God (Ps. 16:11; 21:6). In contrast, the joy of the New Testament takes on a new sense of permanency—

something that continually flows inside of a believer (John 15:11; 1 Thess. 1:6). Far more than coincidence, this subtle change parallels the coming of the Holy Spirit at Pentecost. When the Holy Spirit came to dwell in the hearts of believers, then joy became a fruit of the Spirit and a lasting gift that comes from the presence of God in us.

However, think of the words often used to describe joy — bliss, delight, gladness, contentment, laughter, celebration, and peace. Each of these terms convey emotional or mental states. My delight in worship brings tears to my eyes. I am content when I have confidence in God's leading my life. I celebrate with my neighbor who recently turned his life over to Jesus Christ. Each of these is an expression of biblical joy, but at the same time, you can begin to see why joy and happiness are so easily confused. After all, I also utter these same words to describe states of elation that are slightly less spiritual. I delight in the thought of eating a filet mignon at my favorite steakhouse. I am content with the world after I have my morning cup of coffee. And I celebrate when my New England Patriots win yet another Super Bowl.

Joy is something distinct from these displays of emotion. It's something deeper and more permanent residing inside a believer. Let me illustrate. When I play a music CD in my stereo, there is a difference between the music on the disc and a song that is played at a given moment in time. As a listener, I think of music as the sounds I hear when I play the CD. It's the catchy tune I love to sing along with. But a sound technician understands that the music is actually a stream of audio data that is encoded and pressed onto the surface of the disc. What I am hearing in my ears, the technician would tell me, is the result of the disc's audio information being processed by the CD player.

The distinction between joy and expressions of joy is much like music on my compact disc. Joy lives inside of the spirit of a believer but is revealed through our emotions or states of mind. However, note the difference: these outward manifestations — delight, contentment, and gladness — are not the same as joy itself. Joy is the divine substance underneath.

This CD illustration also helps explain why the emotional highs of joy never last. The audio data stored on a disc is permanently burned onto the CD and never fades away. But a playing of my favorite song takes just four minutes and is then gone forever. Sure, I can always play the tune again, but notice that the playing is a new "expression" of the selection.

In much the same way, expressions of joy don't often last for long in my life. I can be on a spiritual mountaintop after a great worship service. But my elation crashes and burns after I get into a fender bender on the way home. When I look at Scripture, I see that I am not alone. Elijah, for example, rejoiced in the mighty power of God on Mount Carmel on one day, and yet cowardly ran and hid in the desert the next. Joyful expressions come and go quickly, but the joy flowing through my bloodstream never leaves me.

A Choice

Of all of the manifestations of God's love for the world, two stand out in their distinctiveness in the life of a believer: grace and joy. Think of the two as the "twin pillars" of God's amazing love. Grace is a gift that redeems sinners, while joy sustains us in a sinful world. Grace offers us eternity, but joy gives a glimpse of what that eternity will be like. While grace inaugurates our Christian life, joy is its culmination. In describing grace, Philip Yancey says that God "lavished [grace] on those who had in no way earned it, who barely possessed the faculties to receive it." Yancey's description works for joy as well: both grace and joy are free, unearned, and unexpected gifts from God.

Yet while grace and joy are free gifts, I have to choose whether I am going to accept or reject them. Christians know that grace doesn't happen by accident; it enters my life when I choose to repent and believe in the saving work of Jesus Christ. I am discovering that joy works much the same way. The Holy Spirit indwells every believer, but each of us chooses whether or not to live out the joy he offers.

Perhaps the most common response unbelievers have for not accepting Jesus Christ is their belief that they are "good enough" for God to accept them. Back in the 1950s, Bill Bright developed the idea of the Four Spiritual Laws as an evangelism tool to combat this sort of attitude. Bright's vision was to explain, in layman's terms, the basic facts of the gospel and to illustrate the need that every person must make a conscious decision on the gospel. Perhaps the church needs a tract for itself to accomplish a similar task. We need to be reminded that joy never floods into our lives unless we deliberately seek it out.

Unlimited

Because joy is the nature of God flowing inside of me, I can be confident that it will always be available regardless of the sufferings or circumstances I face. As Charles Spurgeon says, "The rill will continue as long as the spring runs; and the joy of a Christian is one that never can alter, because the cause of it never alters."

In the past, when I lumped joy into the same camp as happiness, the apostle James's call to "consider it pure joy" (James 1:2) was a throwaway line to me. Peter's similar encouragement to rejoice in suffering (1 Peter 1:6) also seemed unrealistic in the often nasty and gritty world we live in. But once I realized that my joy isn't human engineered and powered, then these promises of Scripture no longer sounded like fantasy or wishful thinking. My eyes began to open up to the fact that it is more than just theoretically possible to be joyful in all circumstances; it is the only logical conclusion to biblical reality. In fact, this truth ends up looking like something straight out of a Logic 101 class:

My joy is the nature of God living inside of me.

God's nature is unlimited.

Therefore, my joy is unlimited.

Seen in this light, when I fail to tap into the unlimited nature of joy, I become much like a poverty-stricken man who receives an anonymous deposit of billions of dollars into his checking account. Because he has lived hand-to-mouth his entire life, the man has come to dread looking at his account statement. It's just too painful and depressing. So, rather than going through a paper statement each month, he habitually balances his account in his mind, keeping track of his deposits and then living within those constraints. Not surprisingly, when he is slammed by an unexpected medical bill, he stresses out and wonders how he'll ever be able to make the payment.

The irony is that if this man would only recognize his true standing with the bank, his financial life would never be the same again. In fact, he could write check after check for the rest of his life and still never run down his account. God's unlimited supply of joy works this same way. I may impose restraints on God's joy, but these are handcuffs that I put on myself. Or putting it in economic terms, the lack of joy in a believer's life is a demand problem, not a supply problem.

Our Spiritual Lifeblood

In the human body, the heart uses the bloodstream as a delivery mechanism to supply oxygen to all the organs, muscles, and other parts of the body. From a spiritual standpoint, joy is our source and supplier of life. It's our lifeblood, so to speak. "The joy of the LORD is your strength," says Nehemiah (Neh. 8:10). This Old Testament leader is talking about something more than a "sugar rush" or "protein boost" to give us a shot of energy. Instead, I think Nehemiah was hitting at something much deeper. Joy gives us strength, not just to survive but to live meaningful lives. Expanding on Nehemiah, Oswald Chambers says, "The stronghold of the Christian faith is the joy of God, not my joy in God … He reigns and rules and rejoices, and His joy is our strength."

Anemia is a medical condition caused by a lack of iron in a person's body. A person suffering from anemia looks pale and washed out and generally feels lethargic and listless. Christians who live without joy suffer from a spiritual anemia. They are spiritually lifeless, failing to tap into the source of their strength; they exist rather than truly live. Spiritual anemia is so invasive in the life of a believer that it even shows itself in one's physical appearance: an anemic Christian just doesn't have the radiance and vibrancy in his or her countenance as does a joy-filled Christian.

Experienced with Other Believers

One of the tendencies I fight is viewing my faith in solo terms. After all, typical "evangelical-speak" goes something like this: *I make a personal decision for Jesus Christ, and I serve him, following his plan for my life.* Church can be seen as a tangential part of my faith rather than the central role that the New Testament clearly proclaims. Therefore, when I read through each of the passages on joy in the New Testament letters, I was amazed by a clear, consistent theme—joy is experienced primarily with other members of the body of Christ.

The apostle John, for example, indicated that his joy would be "complete" when his readers joined him in fellowship with Christ (1 John 1:4; 2 John 12). Paul seems to go even further. When he talks in personal terms about what gives him joy, he refers to his missionary churches and to other Christian brothers and sisters. The Thessalonians are his "glory and joy" (1 Thess. 2:20). When he prays for the Philippian church, he does so with joy because of their participation in the gospel alongside him (Phil. 1:3). While in prison awaiting possible execution, Paul hopes for a visit from Timothy, who was almost like a son to him, knowing that seeing him will fill him with joy (2 Tim. 1:4). Finally, he tells the Corinthians of the joy he receives because of the concern they have for him (2 Cor. 7:4ff.).

Like the Christian faith as a whole, joy is not a solo act. It is best experienced when you are in intimate fellowship with the body of Christ. The Holy Spirit seems to dispense his joy into our souls the more we love, serve, and fellowship with others.

Rooted in Eternity

My boys and I are avid fans of C. S. Lewis's fantasy series The Chronicles of Narnia. So, when we first got word of the film adaptation of *The Lion, the Witch, and the Wardrobe*, we eagerly anticipated its big-screen release. We regularly scoured the Web for interviews, inside tips from the crew, and other juicy details. My oldest son, Jordan, soon became a regular on a Narnia fan website.

Our excitement peaked when Disney released the film's official trailer several months before the film arrived in theaters. As soon as the trailer became available, my boys and I downloaded it onto our computer and watched it again and again and again. My boys even examined the video clip frame-by-frame to discover details of what the Narnian creatures would look like. The three-minute movie trailer was not satisfying in and of itself, but it offered a taste of what the full-length motion picture was going to be like.

Joy works much the same way—something to be experienced and enjoyed today, but always pointing toward the future. Spurgeon tells us that when we experience joy, "we commence our heaven here below." Peter writes in his first letter of the joy that is rooted in the assurance we have of eternity with Jesus Christ (1 Peter 1:3–7). You can think of joy, therefore, as a taste of heaven while we are living on earth. It's an "otherworldly trailer," previewing the kind of life believers will experience in heaven.

Joy vs. Bizarro Joy

My wife and I recently decided to refinish our pine kitchen table. As the first step, I began sanding down the surface with a belt sander to remove the scratches and old stain finish from the tabletop. However, just as I got underway, I was shocked to discover the pine giving way to corrugated fiberboard underneath. Perhaps I knew years ago that the table was not solid pine, but I had forgotten that information. Now the two of us were stuck with trying to disguise the glaring flaw on the tabletop caused by my sanding.

The veneer-coated table reminded me of the past dabbling I had with happiness — it looks great on the surface, but has no depth and cannot survive the trials of life. The joy I had discovered in the Scriptures looked like a piece of solid wood furniture in comparison. Oh, on the surface, happiness and joy may fool people by looking the same, but these similarities are purely superficial.

The more I grow in my faith, the more I see joy and happiness as opposites rather than like terms. In the comic books, Superman's alter ego is named Bizarro. Happiness now looks much more like "Bizarro joy," an imperfect duplicate of the real thing. Consider how different the two really are from each other.

Happiness is all about the here and now. Biblical joy is rooted in eternity. Happiness is a sound bite that does not last, while joy is like a pleasing chorus that cannot be stopped. "There is no happiness; there are only moments of happiness," says an old Spanish proverb. Joy, on the other hand, combines both: a constant presence of God inside me sprinkled with moments of genuine delight.

Time is the archenemy of happiness, but it is joy's best friend. By its nature, happiness is impatient. Joy, on the other hand, can afford to wait. It knows it has eternity to enjoy.

Happiness depends on circumstances, but joy is independent of anything that happens to me.

Happiness draws me inward to my own personal fulfillment and fills me with more of myself. Filling me with more of Christ, joy turns me outward to God and the world around me. Happiness seeks temporary peace with myself, but joy embraces lasting peace with Jesus Christ.

Pain kills happiness, but joy soothes pain. Not surprisingly, happiness demands that I flee pain at all cost. Joy, by contrast, is open to the suffering that results from obeying Jesus Christ.

"Joy is never in our power and pleasure often is," C. S. Lewis says. That's why, in pursuing happiness, I easily get defensive and bent on protecting the things in my life that make me happy. If Christ leads me away from this end, then I can instinctively become closed-minded to his plans. Biblical joy, by contrast, is open to God's will, even when that call takes me down unhappy roads and gloomy alleyways.

Textures

Texture is a term that often refers to the structure or surface quality of a fabric. Some fabrics are smooth, while others are coarse and open woven. This term has come to be used in a variety of other contexts as well. Great music has texture, not only in the overall sound, but in the depth of the lyrics. The best stories are also sometimes described as having texture. A film like *Snow Falling on Cedars* or a television show like *Lost*, for example, masterfully interweaves multiple plot threads and timing sequences into a unified storyline.

Joy, it seems to me, can only be understood when you realize it has texture too. It has many layers and subtleties. Joy is the nature of God inside of us, but it manifests itself through different emotions, states of mind, and yearnings that penetrate our soul. It is closely intertwined with peace. In fact, it is almost impossible to separate them. Joy can be described as "active peace." Or as an old proverb once described it, "Joy is peace dancing; peace is joy resting." Joy flows from our spirit and floods our heart and mind. It produces deep contentment as we walk with Christ. But it also produces a passionate yearning for something unattainable on this earth.

During my search into the Scriptures for answers, I spent time in the Old Testament, particularly with the joyful expressions scattered throughout the Psalms. I dove into the bold teachings of Peter and James on the subject. I discovered how Paul and John received joy in their fellowship with other believers. But in the end, I found myself always coming back to the Gospels. To me, the books of Matthew, Mark, Luke, and John are the place where the rubber meets the road, where joy must prove its mettle. After all, if joy is all that the Bible purports it to be, then Jesus Christ—literally the God of joy in human flesh—must be the most amazing expression of a joy-filled life that the world has ever seen.

CHAPTER 5

CHRIST OVERJOYED

God, your God, has set you above your companions
by anointing you with the oil of joy.
—Hebrews 1:9

Jesus was a man of such joy, such merriment, such gladness of Spirit,
such freedom and openness, that He was irresistible.
—Sherwood Eliot Wirt

Never underestimate the significance of a single verse in Scripture. Of course, the truth of Christianity rests on the complete record of the Scriptures. There are a handful of "linchpin" verses, however, that seem to stand out in importance. Critical aspects of our faith rest on their shoulders. Verses like Genesis 1:1; 12:1 – 3; Matthew 28:19; and John 14:6 come to mind. Without them, the world and our faith look much different.

When we consider what sort of man Jesus Christ was during his earthly ministry, Hebrews 1:9 is one such linchpin verse: "God, your God, has set you above your companions by anointing you with the oil of joy." This passage dictates the way we should consider the nature of Christ as well as how we should read and understand the four Gospel accounts. The author of Hebrews, drawing from an earlier psalm, tells us that the primary distinguisher of Jesus while on earth was his joy.

If I took a poll among my friends asking them to provide a sound bite description of Jesus Christ, my guess is that I would get responses like: "my risen Savior," "the Son of God," or "the Prince of peace." However, suppose I could go back in time to the first century and ask the contemporaries of Jesus Christ the same question. Based on Hebrews 1:9, I am convinced that the vast majority of his followers would describe him as "a Man of joy."

As relative latecomers to planet Earth, we are introduced to Jesus after his victory on the cross. To us, he is the resurrected Christ, the living Word, and the second person of the Godhead. However, to people who lived with and around him, these sorts of titles were over their heads and not even their concern. Instead, they were far more excited by the kind of man he was on a day-in, day-out basis.

Jesus was something like a rock star once he began his public ministry. A rock-tour-like atmosphere surrounded him on a nearly 24/7 basis. People followed him everywhere. They wanted to hear him speak. They wanted to feel his miraculous touch. As if to emphasize this reality, the Gospels mention specific times in which Christ needed to get away from the crowds and escape into the desert or mountains for time alone to pray.

To attract the masses as he did, most of us simply assume that Jesus Christ was a charismatic preacher with a magnetic personality, or perhaps even one of those "beautiful people" you see pasted on the cover of *People*. After all, if God is going to appear in human flesh once in all of human history, one might expect him to do it with real panache—combining the good looks of Orlando Bloom, the charisma of Johnny Depp, the charm of Pierce Brosnan, and the oratory skills of Kenneth Branagh. However, Scripture actually goes out of its way to say that Jesus was nothing of the sort. In his prophecy on the coming Messiah, the Old Testament prophet Isaiah says:

> *He grew up before him like a tender shoot,*
> *and like a root out of dry ground.*
> *He had no beauty or majesty to attract us to him,*
> *nothing in his appearance that we should desire him.*
> *(Isa. 53:2)*

Jesus, according to Isaiah, was "like a root out of dry ground." In other words, he was not impressive or significant in the eyes of the world. Maybe even a wallflower—overlooked and unnoticed before his ministry started. The prophet adds that Jesus was neither good-looking nor charming. Christ, therefore, had none of the natural human physical or personality characteristics that I would have expected given his messianic role. It's almost as if God went out of his way to make sure that people were not distracted by "Jesus the man," so that he could instead wow the world with his divine joy.

In emphasizing his joy, I am not overlooking the miracles of Jesus. After all, Christ's miraculous power was obviously a major attractor of people. As he traveled throughout ancient Palestine, both the curiosity seekers and the needy sought him out to witness or experience a miracle. Yet while miracles may have produced flocks of people initially, his contagious joy is what kept the crowds following him around day in and day out. To use marketing lingo, the "stickiness" of Jesus Christ's appeal was his joy, not his power.

As an author, one of my greatest loves is communicating through the written word. However, I realize that written communication is not without its shortcomings. Subtleties, attitudes, tones, and emotions are often difficult to convey fully on a piece of paper. Email, in particular, is notorious for this problem. I remember sending off a good-natured ribbing to my friend awhile back. Being friendly banter, I thought nothing of it. However, when he read the email, he completely misunderstood the spirit of the message, since he could not see my smile or hear the friendly tone of my voice. Emoticons—those sideways smiles :-) and frowns :(used to convey emotion and facial gestures—are the postmodern response to this inadequacy of electronic communication.

However, the Bible, at least the TNIV I have beside me on my desk, doesn't make use of emoticons or other such devices. Consequently, when I read an account of Jesus' healing the sick, it may not be immediately obvious whether Jesus did so stoically or with utter delight; the Gospel writers simply didn't provide those kind of details. However, when I read the Gospel accounts in light of Hebrews 1:9—that Christ's joy is what differentiated him from others—I realize that everything Jesus did during his ministry was done with a spirit of joy.

Bruce Marchiano, who portrays Jesus in *The Visual Bible: The Gospel according to Matthew* video, discovered this truth firsthand when researching for his part:

> As I sought to confirm that joy of Jesus in the Word, it became so blatantly obvious I couldn't believe I never

caught it before. Suddenly, it was everywhere, screaming from the pages of Scripture: joy!... Jesus began jumping off of the page at me as well—His realness and strength, the sparkle in His eyes, the spring in His gait, the heartiness in His laugh, the genuineness of His touch; His passion, playfulness, excitement, and vitality: His joy!

In *The Gospel according to Matthew*, Bruce depicts Jesus as a man of joy—wholly unlike the somber, detached versions of Christ in other films over the years. In fact, Bruce's portrayal of Jesus had a profound effect on my faith when I first viewed the video. For in watching this four-hour, word-by-word account of the Gospel of Matthew, I began to grasp the reality of a joyful Jesus in a way that I never realized before.

Perhaps the scene in this video that most effectively captures the essence of Christ's joy is the story of the leper's healing in Matthew 8:1 – 3. When I read the passage in my Bible, I tend to focus on the nuts and bolts of the brief encounter: a leper meets Jesus; Jesus miraculously heals the leper; the leper goes off a healed man. However, when you see the scene visually acted out before you, you start to understand the sort of joyous interaction that must have taken place between the two men. The video's director, Regardt van den Bergh, recalled the thoughts that went through his mind when filming the scene:

> I felt compelled by the Lord that Jesus should go on His knees, the healed man should fall into His arms, and together they should roll in the dust. My immediate reaction was "No, I can't do that!" but I obeyed, and that scene became one of the most popular scenes in the whole production. Through the eyes of religion we tend

to see Jesus as thus an extremely reserved and serene figure—the Son of God who would never show so much joy as to burst into laughter and roll in the dust at a leper's healing. But the Lord led us to bring joy to the character of Jesus.

Jesus Christ was the ultimate conduit of heavenly joy. According to the apostle Paul in Romans 8, all of creation "groans" in anticipation for the future second coming of Christ. Perhaps the reason creation so eagerly waits is because of the glorious joy it witnessed during Christ's coming the first time around.

But what about the rest of us? Can we radiate joy like Christ?

CHAPTER 6

LUMPS OF SUNSHINE

What a lump of sunshine that man was!
—Charles Spurgeon

From his whole person,
joy seemed to radiate.
—*Les Misérables*

Talking with Clint always invigorates me. More than any other person I've met in my life, Clint radiates the joy that is so uniquely Christian. I first met Clint when Kimberly and I moved to Washington, D.C., so I could attend graduate school. He was an elder at our new church and led a Bible study for young married couples at his home each Wednesday. Clint wasn't a dynamic speaker or a charismatic man. But he possessed a gentle spirit, thoughtful wisdom, and a childlike enthusiasm for life that made people want to just be around him.

Clint had begun working as a senior staffer in a powerful lobbying firm on Capitol Hill. As an impressionable graduate student who wanted to be in the same field, his prestigious position may have been the initial draw I had to the man. But as time went on, I became attracted to another part of him that was far more significant.

One Wednesday evening when we arrived at his home for Bible study, Clint told us that he had resigned from his position earlier that day following a dispute with the head of the firm. It was a matter of conscience, he said. In spite of the unexpected blow to his career, Clint had amazing peace about the whole thing. He then started on a job search that would stretch from days, to weeks, to months. Eventually, being unable to find another Capitol Hill job, he took a janitorial position at a local Christian school.

His career took a nosedive in a matter of months, but his joy was constant throughout. At Bible study each week, he'd give us an update on his job status, but no matter how discouraging the news was, he always had a peace in his heart and a radiant smile on his face. He wasn't just putting on an act either; he was being real. In fact, he was candid about how humbling it was for him to accept a job as a janitor after his long, proficient career in management. But in spite of that humiliation, he was able to hand all of those issues off to God and delight in him anyway.

Clint is retired now and lives a thousand miles from where I live. However, as a father figure of sorts to me, he continues to keep in touch. And each time we connect, I still sense that same joyful, exuberant, Spirit-filled man that he always was.

The Pleasantville Effect

Old Faithful is the most celebrated of all geysers. Located in Yellowstone National Park, Old Faithful shoots thousands of gallons of boiling water high into the air every hour and a half. This hydrogeological activity is caused by underground water streams coming into contact with molten rock. A mixture of superhot water and steam forms from the collision, gradually building up tremendous amounts of pressure. Eventually, when the steam pressure is too strong to be held back, a jet of steam and water shoots to the surface.

Joy flows from the heart of a Christian much like Old Faithful does at Yellowstone. The divine nature of God rushes through a believer's bloodstream; when it collides with a thirsty, seeking heart, the mixture produces a heavenly joy so potent that it cannot be contained inside any human fixture. "True joy, when it is joy in the Lord, must speak," preached Charles Spurgeon; "it cannot hold its tongue, it must praise the Lord."

The "Pleasantville Effect" is a film technique made popular by movies such as *Pleasantville* and *Schindler's List*. The visual effect is simple, but powerful—an entire scene is filmed in black-and-white, except for a single object that is shown in color. A viewer's eyes can't help but be drawn to the lone color figure on the screen. Steven Spielberg, for example, brilliantly used this technique in *Schindler's List*. In a brutal scene in which Nazi soldiers take over a Warsaw ghetto, the camera follows a small Jewish girl wearing a candy red coat. Even when the camera pans to a wide shot showing at least one hundred other people, the red coat draws the viewer to her. This colorful image of the girl stands in stark contrast to the chaos all around.

In a world of letdown and disillusionment, joy produces a "Pleasantville Effect" on the life of a believer. The contentment, liveliness, peace, and vibrancy that come from joy cause the joyous Christian to stand apart from others around him. Spurgeon put it like this:

> When joy comes into a man, it shines out of his eyes, it sparkles in his countenance. There is something about every limb of the man that betokens that his body, like a well-tuned harp, has had its strings put in order. Joy—it refreshes the marrow of the bones; it quickens the flowing of the blood in the veins.

Just as a film viewer is drawn to a colorized figure in a black-and-white scene, I find myself naturally attracted to a Christian filled with joy. I want to hang around that person. I want to have that joy. Spurgeon describes a similar reaction that he had to a man in his church nicknamed Old Father Dransfield: "What a lump of sunshine that man was!... The very sight of him seemed to fill me with exhilaration, for his joy was wholly in his God!"

A lump of sunshine. What a wonderful description of an earnest believer! Packing the very nature of God, the joy-filled Christian can't help but radiate sunshine across the world's monochromatic landscape.

An Apostle of Joy

The apostle Paul is arguably the most influential theologian of all time. He authored nearly half of the New Testament, and his letter to the Romans is considered by many scholars as the definitive work on Christian theology. As the apostle to the Gentiles, Paul successfully planted and discipled many churches scattered throughout the Roman empire.

In order for Paul to have achieved all that he did, one might guess that he possessed a rare aura and charisma to win converts and attract people far and wide. But Paul had nothing of the sort. In fact, the only thing Paul had to win people over was a life that radiated the joy of Christ.

The Scriptures are pretty candid that Paul was not an attractive or striking individual. In a culture that placed tremendous value on classical rhetoric and oratory skills, Paul was a mediocre preacher. He writes to the Corinthian church that he came to them "in weakness with great fear and trembling" (1 Cor. 2:3 – 4a). Some even complained that his writings were powerful, but "in person he is unimpressive and his speaking amounts to nothing" (2 Cor. 10:10). And, in what can be seen as an almost comical story in Acts, his preaching was evidentally dull enough to put a boy to sleep, causing him to fall out of a second-story window (Acts 20:7 – 11).

Paul was not impressive to look at. Early Christian sources, in fact, suggest that he was short, balding, and perhaps even hunchbacked from his beatings. He was also plagued by a physical problem that Paul himself admits was a distraction to others when he was with them.

Paul appears to have had a blustery and fiery personality, at least on occasion. Some in the Corinthian church, in fact, wrote him off as something of a buffoon.

And yet how the churches adored Paul! I recently read through all of Paul's letters during one sitting, and what stood out as much as his teaching was the intimate relationship he had with his churches. He saw himself much like a compassionate, love-struck father to these believers; the churches and his fellow workers responded with a remarkable love and loyalty to him.

What makes this attraction to Paul even more amazing is that he was an itinerant pastor. Traveling missionaries and pastors can have an impact on a church congregation for the time that they are physically there with them, but most are usually forgotten about as soon as they leave town. Not so with Paul. The New Testament churches were constantly urging Paul to visit them again. When he was imprisoned and unable to come, they sent letters and emissaries to encourage him. The Galatians were a church willing to do anything for Paul. He even remarks that if they would have been able to, they would have pulled out their eyes and given them to him (Gal. 4:15). Priscilla and Aquila risked their lives for Paul (Rom. 16:3–4), and Christian worker Epaphroditus almost worked himself to death so he could participate with Paul in his ministry (Phil. 2:25–30).

The first chapter of Philippians might be the most revealing passage of all concerning the nature of Paul's ministry. It reveals a special bond and deep affection between Paul and the church in Philippi. Paul says in verses 4–8:

> In all my prayers for all of you, I always pray with joy because of your partnership in the gospel from the first day until now ... It is right for me to feel this way about all of you, since I have you in my heart and, whether I am in chains or defending and confirming the gospel, all of you share in God's grace with me. God can testify how I long for all of you with the affection of Christ Jesus.

I can imagine that there are only a handful of pastors of churches today who even approach this sort of intimacy with their congregations.

"For when I am weak, then I am strong," Paul told the Corinthian church (2 Cor. 12:10). Paul's joy in Christ was his strength that enabled him to conquer his glaring human weaknesses and become a most beloved shepherd.

Radiating Joy

Monseigneur Bienvenu is a character who plays a small but pivotal role as the bishop in the classic novel *Les Misérables*. In fact, if you've seen the film or musical adaptation of the Victor Hugo epic, you probably do not even know his name.

Les Misérables tells the story of how a simple act of grace by Bienvenu transforms the life of a hardened convict named Jean Valjean. As the story unfolds, the newly paroled Valjean is looking for a place to lodge while passing through a small town. After he is turned away by all of the inns, he decides to knock on the door of a bishop's parsonage.

The bishop welcomes Valjean into his home like a brother, feeding him a hot meal and offering a warm bed for the night. But being jaded by his years spent in the penitentiary, Valjean is less than grateful for the kindness shown. Needing cash, Valjean rises in the middle of the night and runs off with the bishop's silverware. The convict does not get very far, however; he is caught red-handed with the stolen goods by the police as he attempts to flee town.

When the police bring Valjean back to the bishop's home for questioning, Valjean expects the worst. He knows that if he is found guilty of the crime, his sentence will be life in prison. He is, therefore, dumbstruck when the bishop dismisses the police, telling them that the silver was a gift. Bienvenu's grace doesn't stop there; he places two silver candlesticks, the only possessions of value he owns, into Valjean's knapsack. "Jean Valjean, my brother," says the bishop with a joyful gleam in his eye, "you belong no longer to evil, but to good. It is your soul I am buying for you. I withdraw it from the dark thoughts ... and I give it to God!"

If you've seen a film or musical adaptation of *Les Misérables*, that is all you really learn about the bishop. The story moves on to focus on the new life of Valjean. However, if you read the unabridged version of the Victor Hugo novel, you are able to discover much more about who this man really was. Bienvenu proves to be more than just a kindly old priest. Instead, he proves to be a beaming man of joy.

Bienvenu's entire life is dedicated to serving Jesus Christ and others around him. When he first arrives in town to accept the bishop's appointment, he is given a grand, spacious mansion in which to live. But after seeing the needs of a cramped hospital next door, he claims there must be a mistake and promptly trades places with the hospital. "You have my house and I have yours," he tells the hospital director. "Restore me to mine; you are at home." Later, when affluent members of his congregation have given funds for a new altar in his oratory, he takes the money and gives it to the poor in the area instead. While many people around him spend their lives trying to mine for riches, he works, in Hugo's words, "for the extraction of pity."

Bienvenu is a good shepherd of his flock. When he has money, he visits the poor. When he is broke, he makes a pastoral visit to the rich. In caring for others, he always seems to know the appropriate response. He can sit for hours in complete silence alongside a widower who has just lost his wife, while on another occasion he is active in fervent prayer with a dying man on a hospital bed.

The entire town adores the bishop. Their attraction isn't based on his looks, his charm, or even his caretaking. Instead, it is that "indefinable something" he possesses. "From his whole person," wrote Hugo, "joy seemed to radiate."

Beyond Prince Charming

Jesus was no Prince Charming; Isaiah tells us as much. Neither was Paul or Monseigneur Bienvenu. But oftentimes, I think we look for one today. As a culture, we are naturally attracted to people with charisma and charm. The endless fascination of Hollywood stars in the media is clear evidence of that fact. In some ways, I think this attraction spills over into the church as well. Today's Christian leaders are dynamic and personable men and women. They are the heads of megachurches, regularly appear on Christian television and radio, and are the headline speakers at the conferences we attend. Even in my local church, the people I see in the most visible roles are those with dynamic personalities.

My wife and I had dinner recently with a group of people from our church. During the course of the evening, the topic of conversation turned to a nice-looking young couple who just joined our congregation and was getting involved in various ministries. In sitting back and listening to the discussion, I was struck that all of the enthusiasm for the couple seemed to be based on their charisma and sophisticated looks. I began to wonder if the same enthusiasm would have been shown to a shy, homely-looking couple who had the same heart for Christ. I suspect not.

There is nothing wrong with charisma, of course. After all, this human trait is a gift from God. However, we need to make sure we don't use it as a measuring stick for Christian maturity. Charisma has nothing to do with a person's spiritual state, but joy is a direct result of it. A person can put on charm; no one can really fake joy. In the words of Oswald Chambers, "The one thing that Jesus Christ does for a man is to make him radiant, not artificially radiant. There is nothing more irritating than the counsel, 'keep smiling.' That is a counterfeit, a radiance that soon fizzles out."

When charisma is the sole attraction you have toward a person, you will eventually come away feeling unimpressed or even disillusioned. Back when I was in high school, a dynamic speaker came to my church for a special youth weekend retreat. I was totally mesmerized by his preaching. And like any hero worshiper, I wanted to get to know him and be known by him as well. When I interacted with the man at a later time, however, I discovered he was not the person I expected. He seemed, to me anyway, a fake, a paper-thin shell of the man I heard preaching.

In contrast, the more time you spend with a joy-filled believer, the more your attraction will grow for that person. Take, for example, Monseigneur Bienvenu in *Les Misérables*. Hugo wrote that the first impression that people had on meeting him was dismissive: just a nice guy with a ho-hum personality. However, the more people got to know him, the more they developed an undeniable attraction toward the man. Hugo describes:

> At the first view, and to one who saw him for the first time, he was nothing more than a good man. But if one spent a few hours with him ... little by little the good man became transfigured, and became ineffably imposing ... majesty was developed from this goodness, yet the radiance of goodness remained; and one felt something of the emotion that he would experience in seeing a smiling angel slowly spread his wings without ceasing to smile. Respect, unutterable respect, penetrated you by degrees, and made its way to your heart; and you felt that you had before you one of those strong, tried, and indulgent souls, where the thought is so great that it cannot be other than gentle.

A man or woman who possesses joy has a raw power that goes beyond charisma and charm. Penetrating the souls of people they came into contact with, their "weight of joy" becomes a commanding force that God uses to draw others to himself.

Race of Truth

I want to do more than hang out with my friend Clint or read about people like Paul or Bienvenu. *I want to be like them.* When I interact with others, I yearn for them to see joy flowing out of me too. I want them to walk away from me with a contagious desire for the joy of the Lord, that same sort of thing I experienced when I spent anytime at all with Clint. I don't say this out of ego or pride, but purely out of the realization that that's the sort of life God designed me to live.

However, I know that far too much of the joy that God packs inside of me never flows outside. I have a nasty habit of hoarding it. Rather than seeking out the needs of others, I let the busyness of the day preoccupy my mind. My natural shyness can hinder me from interacting with people I don't know well. Bienvenu remarks in *Les Misérables*, "I am not in the world to care for my life, but for souls." Sadly, all too often, I think I am in the world to push my own petty agenda rather than simply loving and serving the people around me. But when I do so, the "Pleasantville Effect" around me no longer works. The joy that should distinguish me fades into the black-and-white background of the world.

The Tour de France is one of my favorite sporting events to watch on television. Each July, two hundred bicycle racers race two thousand miles over twenty days all around the French countryside and mountains. During the opening flat stages of the race, it is often difficult to distinguish between the contenders and the pretenders. The majority of the riders, including all of the race favorites, will stick together in the *peloton* (the main pack), while a handful of lesser riders break away, hoping for a single day's stage victory. Often, one of these breakaway riders will gain enough time on the rest of the field to take the *maillot jeune* (the leader's jersey) away from the race favorites for a few days.

However, at the end of the week, the Tour schedules an individual time trial, a race in which a cyclist races by himself against the clock. Among race enthusiasts, the time trial is nicknamed the "race of truth," because no rider can simply "hide" in the *peloton* or use some cheeky tactic to gain time on others. Instead, by day's end, the clock reveals exactly which individuals are actually contending for the Tour victory and which are not.

The tell-all nature of the time trial reminds me of the way in which the display of joy in my life reveals what is going on in my soul. It's a public test of truth indicating where I stand with Jesus Christ. People will either see joy flowing or they won't.

When the nature of God is in control of a person's life, joy cannot help but spill out. However, because we live in a sinful world, other factors can easily bottleneck joy and hinder it from surfacing. Some people are prone to worrying, stressing out, and getting angry. Others have past baggage that so dominates their present life that they can't see beyond it. These strongholds can make it difficult for the person to exhibit much joy at all.

When I was growing up, I attended vacation Bible school during summer break. One of the songs we'd sing each year was "This Little Light of Mine." "This little light of mine, I'm gonna let it shine," goes the tune over and over. Most adults listening to it probably consider it trite and simplistic. It's a children's song, after all. However, when I listen to the words carefully, I begin to realize that this song offers insight into the way true joy is expressed in our lives. All believers are equipped with a light inside of them, enabling them to radiate joy to the rest of the world. However, as the song indicates, it is still my choice whether I am going to let it shine in my life. I can hide it under a bushel. I can let Satan blow it out. Or I can be a lump of sunshine.

My head knew what kind of joy I wanted and what kind I did not. My heart longed to outwardly radiate it to the rest of the world. But one nagging question remained: How do I actually receive this lasting joy and experience it daily in my Christian walk?

PART 3

LIVING JOY

CHAPTER 7

THE "S" WORD

We have dragged down the idea of surrender and of sacrifice,
we have taken the life out of the words
and made them mean something sad and weary and despicable;
in the Bible they mean the very opposite.

—Oswald Chambers

The soul is but a hollow which God fills.

—C. S. Lewis

Walking the plank. That's how I have often described my life over the past three years. I exchanged the security of a regular paycheck with the uncertainty of eking out a living with my pen. With three rapidly growing boys and a new mortgage, what was I thinking? In what should have been the most risk-averse phase of my life, I was risking an awful lot. Was this all just "Rich's folly"? Was I walking hand in hand with my family off the edge of the plank into the ocean waters below?

Life as a writer was turning into a thrashing sea of circumstances. Up and down. Up and down. I would get excited about a promising book opportunity, only to see it fizzle out before anything came of it. We'd rejoice in making the month's mortgage payment only to have our aging minivan break down on the highway the next day. I spent six intensive months writing the best manuscript I'd ever done, only to see the publisher pull the plug before they had even seen my work. We were surviving, but I felt as each day went by that we were creeping ever closer to the plank's edge.

During this same period, God was also dealing with me in other areas of my life. The Old Testament prophet Malachi talks about God being a refiner's fire, burning off all impurities in our lives. I was feeling the heat all around me. My wife and I struggled as we worked through some tough, longstanding issues in our marriage. As a father, I wrestled with decisions over how I should divide my time among career, ministry, and family. My faith felt as if it was being stretched, torn, and reassembled on a daily basis.

But something was different inside of me as I went through these storms. I was not getting stressed out, panic-stricken, or even moody. I was actually experiencing joy! I had a newfound calmness and sense of peace in the midst of the trials. People like to associate God's blessing with good circumstances and happy times. I disagree. I felt his blessing when I was facing the very real prospects of professional failure and a zero balance bank account.

Oh, I still had bouts of doubt and periods where I didn't feel much joy at all. But these periods were less frequent and the recovery time was much faster. Overall, the joy I was experiencing was measurably different from anything I had experienced before. Had I finally discovered a bridge across my joy gap? If so, what was it?

A Mysterious Connection

The "S" word. For much of my life, I found myself subconsciously treating it like a swear word—something to avoid dwelling upon if I could help it. The "S" word is a basic teaching of Jesus Christ, but it is a topic you never see on top of the Christian book bestseller charts. The church gives lip service to the "S" word, but we have a hard time actually living it out in our daily lives. The word I am speaking of is, of course, *surrender.*

Surrender means that I give up my interests, agenda, priorities, and needs and hand them all over to Jesus Christ. This deliberate, decisive action is at the heart of what discipleship is all about. Jesus tells us so in Mark 8:34 – 35, "Whoever wants to be my disciple must deny themselves and take up their cross and follow me. For whoever wants to save their life will lose it, but whoever loses their life for me and for the gospel will save it." As I read this passage, I can't help but think that Jesus would have made a lousy salesman or marketing exec. Notice the sobering nature of the verbs he uses: deny yourself, take up your cross, follow him to Golgotha, and lose your life. In *The Cost of Discipleship*, Dietrich Bonhoeffer puts Christ's call in even more stark terms: "When Jesus calls a man he bids him 'come and die.'"

Since most of us are not going to die martyrs' deaths, the apostle Paul helps us get practical by urging us to offer up ourselves as "living sacrifices" to God. In Judaism, a sacrifice was a most sacred act performed to symbolize the cost of sin and our need for atonement. A sacrificed animal was killed and cut into pieces, and then parts were thrown into a fire. The burnt pieces were placed on the altar and offered to God by the offender or the priest. Therefore, to become a living sacrifice, I figuratively throw myself into the fire and then place the remnants on the altar as an offering. Seen in this light, surrender is more than just giving up sin; it is giving up any claim I have to myself.

Burnt offerings. Living sacrifices. Carrying crosses. That's tough stuff. Surrender ends up sounding like something akin to a trip to the dentist for a root canal—necessary, but utterly painful. Since pain is something we instinctively avoid, it is not surprising that surrender becomes much like a swear word to us.

Some time ago, a friend of my wife gave a copy of Andrew Murray's *Absolute Surrender* to us to read. She was raving over the classic book, telling us of the significant impact that it had on her faith. I was excited for her and nodded in affirmation, but then proceeded to place the book on the shelf and leave it there. Every so often, I'd pass the book and say to myself, "I *really* do need to read that." But it was nearly a year later before I actually picked it up. As I reflected on why it took so long for me to open up the cover, I realized that it wasn't that I didn't want to be challenged. My hesitation was based on the notion that the whole subject matter sounded so joyless and uninviting. Reading about absolute surrender sounded like absolute drudgery.

Perception and reality are often much different, however. As I reflected on the storms I was facing in my life, my experience was proving this whole "swear word perception" entirely wrong. I was surrendering more of myself to Christ, yet I was experiencing more joy than ever before. Perhaps this was not just a strange coincidence. Maybe there was actually some mysterious relationship between surrender and joy. For the first time, surrender no longer sounded like a death march, but a journey to joy.

Lessons from Punxsutawney

My decade-long search for joy is reminiscent of the journey that Phil Connors takes in the 1993 romantic comedy *Groundhog Day*. In the film, TV weatherman Connors arrives in the small Pennsylvania town of Punxsutawney to report on the annual Groundhog Day festivities. After a sudden snowstorm forces the cynical and unbearable Connors and his crew to stay in town an extra night, Phil wakes up the next morning to discover that something very strange has happened. Déjà vu—it's Groundhog Day all over again. When the same thing happens on the following day and then the next, Phil realizes that he is helplessly stuck, reliving the second day of February over and over and over in Punxsutawney.

Phil is initially convinced he is going crazy. But after he gets used to the situation, he adapts and actually begins to enjoy himself. After all, since there are no long-term consequences to his actions, he can do whatever he pleases. Munching down a table full of high-calorie desserts. Chasing after women. Stealing money. Taking the police on a wild-goose chase around town. Anything goes, because when he wakes up the next morning, it is as if nothing has happened. Yet as time goes on, Phil realizes that none of these guilty pleasures satisfy him. So he sets his sights on conquering his coworker, Rita. After she sees through his slick romancing attempts day after day, however, he ends up completely hopeless.

As the months drag on, his attitude becomes bleaker and bleaker. In the monotony of constantly reliving the same day, he begins to lose all reason to live — so much so that he tries to take his own life several times. But no matter what he does to himself, Phil wakes up the next morning "without a dent in the fender" and as healthy as ever.

As the story continues, Connors finally comes to the end of himself. Hitting rock bottom, he slowly begins a transformation into a new man. After a lifetime of selfishness and cynicism, he realizes that pursuing his own selfish interests only leads him to despair. However, when he forgets about himself and lives for others, life begins to have a new purpose and hope.

For most of my life, I was like Phil Connors. I tried a variety of ways to discover joy on my own terms. I was living for Christ, but not giving up all the rights to myself. Growing up, I was the good guy who followed all of the rules. In college, I was the theologian, studying and learning all I could about the Christian faith. My rebellious phase took me deep into the world to explore earthly happiness as a substitute. Once I was back on track, I became the Promise Keeper, trying to balance work, family, and church ministries. However, as I've already shared, none of these produced joy that lasted or endured. It was not until after I'd exhausted my own solutions that Christ supplied his own and on his own terms.

Groundhog Day may be intended as a heartwarming, fun film, but I consider it more than that: it is a vivid reminder of a fundamental Christian truth — humans are incapable of experiencing meaning and joy unless we fully give up our claim to ourselves and live for Christ and others around us.

Empty Mugs

The intimate connection between surrender and joy was hard for me to believe initially. After all, for most of my life, the two almost seemed as if they belonged on opposite sides of the faith spectrum. Surrender was gritty—obedience, discipleship, and the cross; joy was about delight—peace, celebration, and hope. But as I started to consider what joy really is—the nature of God flowing through my spiritual bloodstream—then the mystery not only started to make sense, but emerged as the only real way to experience joy that lasts.

Consider, after all, the parallels with an actual human circulatory system. When a person has high levels of cholesterol, a hard, pasty substance forms on the artery walls and slowly narrows the passageway of the arteries. Over a period of years, the buildup can become so severe that a clot forms and prevents the blood from flowing through—leading to a heart attack. Just as cholesterol can block the blood flow into my heart, my claim to myself obstructs the Holy Spirit from working in my life. However, when I surrender all, then my spiritual arteries are opened, so to speak, and his joy is able to flow abundantly through me.

Jesus Christ backs this up when he delivers his great promise of joy in John 15:11: "I have told you this so that my joy may be in you and that your joy may be complete." Notice that his promise doesn't stand on its own, however. Jesus links his promise of joy to "this"—the sermon he has delivered in the first fourteen verses of the chapter. When you look at what Jesus has been talking about in this passage, his message amounts to call to all-out surrender—remain true and steadfast in him and live in full obedience to his Word. Seen in light of John 15, joy is not a "Shangri La," an elusive, mystical destination reserved for spiritual gurus. Instead, joy is the natural result of any believer who earnestly follows Christ's commands.

Jesus wasn't just pushing off the cause-and-effect nature of surrender and joy to his followers either. Hebrews 12:2 tells us, "For the joy set before him he endured the cross." Yes, even Jesus Christ himself experienced joy as he sacrificed himself for the sins of the world.

Joy's dependence on surrender closely parallels grace's dependence on repentance. Both grace and joy require a deliberate action in order to receive them: to accept God's grace, I repent; to accept his joy, I surrender. On first take, repentance and surrender sound an awful lot like strict demands from an overbearing Lord. Nothing, however, is further from the truth. C. S. Lewis points out that repentance "is not something God demands of you before He will take you back ... it is simply a description of what going back is like." In the same way, when we understand what joy really is, the need for surrender becomes rather obvious: God's joy is only possible to experience when I get rid of all the personal stuff in its way.

Consider an everyday example to bring this reality home. I am a coffee fanatic, and one of my favorite delights is drinking a cup of Ethiopian Harrar, a rare coffee bean that is usually available for a season every other year. Suppose my wife secretly buys a pound of Harrar and brews a pot of it for me. She then comes into my office to fill up my mug, only to discover it is already filled with lukewarm coffee from earlier in the day. My wife is ready to pour me the good stuff, but in order to do that, she tells me I must dump out my old cupful first. My wife is obviously not being overbearing or arbitrary in her demand. It is simply a matter of common sense: the Harrar brew *cannot* be poured into a cup already filled. Similarly, Christ's joy can't be poured into a life filled with personal leftovers.

In the end, I discovered that surrender is not a miserable act at all. Instead, it becomes my way out of misery. Rather than giving up my identity, surrender actually enhances it. To paraphrase C. S. Lewis, when God talks about my losing myself, he only means abandoning the clamor of self-will; once I have done that, he really gives me back all my personality, and he promises that when I am wholly his, I will be more myself than ever. That's the blessed promise of joy.

Tweeners

If I had been alive during Jesus' earthly ministry and followed him around, I am sure I would have considered Peter to be my role model for living a surrendered life. Peter, after all, was the gung-ho disciple, the most loyal and diehard of them all. He was the only one of the twelve who attempted to walk on the water toward Jesus. He was the first disciple to proclaim Jesus as the "Son of God." The ever-confident Peter told Jesus just before his arrest, "Even if I have to die with you, I will never disown you" (Matt. 26:35). And yet, hours after making that bold statement, Peter failed miserably; his brash talk and attitude drowned in a pool of bitter tears. Peter had not yet reached the point where he was willing to give himself up fully to God.

Peter was what I call a "tweener" during that season of his life. A tweener is a believer who lives an in-between stage — wanting to live for Christ, but either unwilling to hand over all of oneself or feeling unable to do so.

Looking at the church today, I believe it is filled with far too many tweeners. We can boldly sing the praise song "I Surrender All" in a worship service, all the while having no clue whatsoever of the implications of what we are singing about. Oswald Chambers points out that "there is no bigger word and no word made more shallow than surrender. To say 'I surrender all' may be blathering sentiment, or it may be the deep passionate utterance of the life."

"Just how *absolute* is absolute surrender?" we ask. After all, Jesus commands me to take up my cross and follow him. However, in one sense, this call cannot be taken literally — I am not going to pick up an actual wooden cross and carry it down around the town square to my crucifixion. As a result, I often found it easy to unconsciously treat Jesus' symbolism as an excuse to water down the message. His call became mere sentiment. Consequently, I ended up twisting Paul's idea of a "living sacrifice, holy and pleasing to God" into my idea of a "convenient sacrifice, wholly pleasing to myself."

But when Jesus calls me to surrender everything to him, he means it. He wants us to listen, obey, and then get on with it. Bonhoeffer illustrates this point through a simple story. Suppose a father sends his son off to bed. The boy knows exactly what the intentions of his father are, but imagine the child rationalizing the way we often do with God. He might argue something like this: "My dad tells me to go to bed, but what he really means is that I am sleepy, and he does not want me to be tired. However, I can overcome my tiredness just as well if I go out and play. So, though dad tells me to go to bed, he really is saying: 'Go out and play.'"

The rich young ruler in Mark 10 is one tweener who clearly understood the implications of Jesus' specific call to him: "Go, sell everything you have and give to the poor, and you will have treasure in heaven. Then come, follow me" (v. 21). Judging by the man's reaction, we can be certain that he knew exactly what Jesus was calling him to do. Jesus was not being an idealist, he was being extremely practical. Christ knew this specific, decisive action was the only thing that would cause true surrender in the man's heart. Sadly, the young ruler rides joylessly away, realizing that he was not prepared to truly abandon everything he had for Christ.

Besides treating Christ's words as an ideal, tweeners can also reduce the impact of Jesus' call by giving only part of themselves to Christ. The Sunday morning chorus "I Surrender All" becomes "I Surrender Parts" by the afternoon, as we pick and choose what compartments of our lives we will give up. A missionary to Africa may "abandon it all" for his profession and ministry. But he may struggle with anger and selfishness around his family and be hardened to doing anything about it. Or consider an executive who has the gift of evangelism and senses a call to full-time ministry. He preaches every chance he gets at his church and volunteers twice a month at the local soup kitchen. However, he is so fearful of quitting his comfortable, safe job and being unable to provide for his family that he dismisses the call to the ministry.

Some tweeners, however, experience an altogether opposite reaction. Rather than treating Christ's call lightly or reducing it, they become so overwhelmed that they feel powerless to actually pull it off. Surrender may be the journey to joy, but to this tweener, it sounds like an impassible mountain ascent.

Turning back to the Gospels, Christ himself says in Matthew 11:30, "My yoke is easy and my burden is light." Perhaps Christ is just being overly optimistic. Or perhaps he is driving at a key truth of surrender: I have to make a decision on my own to surrender everything to him. But I am *not* alone in actually carrying it out. God accomplishes the surrender in our lives as we are open to him. We achieve it in his strength. As Hebrews 11:34 says, we gain strength in weakness as we empty ourselves for him—not only in our hearts but in our livelihoods as well.

CHAPTER 8

DRIVEN BY PURPOSE

God made me for a purpose — for China.
But he also made me fast — and when I run, I feel his pleasure.
To give it up would be to hold him in contempt;
to win is to honor him.
—Eric Liddell, *Chariots of Fire*

A poor maid should have the joy in her heart of being able to say:
"Now I am cooking, making the bed, sweeping the house ...
How could I possibly be more blessed?
Why, my service is equal to cooking for God in heaven!"
—Martin Luther

"What a waste," my friend Mitch said to me as we sat down for our regular Wednesday lunch.

"What's wrong?" I asked.

"I just spent an entire morning trying to win back a customer whom my boss ticked off. What's the point?"

"Yeah, I pulled my second all-nighter in a week making sure our 5.0 release is ready. The depressing thing, though, is not the effort involved, but the feeling that none of this matters."

"How so?"

"Internet software ... the crazy stuff goes obsolete so quickly. Mark my words, in two years' time, people will have moved on to something else."

"There has to be—" Mitch paused as he bit into his sandwich—"more to my life than just selling copiers and saving my boss's hide once a week."

Nodding, I responded, "Where's your heart?"

"Ministry. That's my real joy."

"Yeah, I want to write."

Back when I lived in Silicon Valley, Mitch and I met each week at a small deli in Redwood City. Over soup and a sandwich, we shared our dreams and goals and wrestled with how to follow God's plan for our lives. After forty-five minutes, we'd usually give up trying to figure everything out, grab a Starbucks Venti, and head back to work.

Mitch and I were at a similar stage in life. We were both working in jobs we believed God provided and called us to. But neither of us considered what we were doing as our "life's purpose." Gifted as a shepherd and counselor, Mitch wanted to enter the ministry. I wanted to be a writer. Both of us were driven by something deep inside of us to do what we believed we were created to do.

What is the purpose of my life? Does God have a personal plan for me? Why am I here? Mitch and I are not alone in asking these sorts of questions. The blockbuster success of Rick Warren's *Purpose Driven Life* shows just how deep-seated these questions are—not only within the church, but outside of it as well. Every person wants—no, needs—a purpose. A purpose is commonly thought of as what we actively pursue with our time, whether it is a healthy family life, a challenging career, a church ministry, or a beloved hobby. When people have a purpose, they find meaning and hope; people without purpose can feel so empty inside that they eventually lose even the desire to live.

The pursuit of joy in our life is tightly interwoven with our purpose. God created the human race to have an intimate relationship with him; I experience joy through that spiritual intimacy when I surrender myself to his will. But he designed us with two hands, two feet, and an ever-active mind. Clearly, he also prepared us from the very beginning to experience joy when we do the activities that he wants us to—such as building, creating, caring, cultivating, and teaching. God, it seems, not only designed us to be joyful in spirit, but also joyful in action.

Earlier in the book, I talked about how everyone, regardless of their faith, can discover a "common joy" in music, art, or nature. I think that same idea applies to work as well. I am reminded of a scene in the 1981 film *Chariots of Fire* in which runner Harold Abrahams and his date, singer Sybil Gordon, are discussing their careers and what motivates them. Harold asks Sybil, "Why singing?"

She replies, "It's my job." Then, after thinking about the question more, she corrects herself, saying, "No, that's silly; I do it because I love it." Sybil's response reveals an underlying truth of God's design for humankind: believers and nonbelievers alike experience God's "common joy" when we do something we are good at.

Just having a purpose isn't enough, however, to experience the lasting joy that Christ promises us in John 15. I know many people who are consumed by purpose and love their jobs, but who lead miserable lives. Even Hugh Heffner, Fidel Castro, and Donald Trump have purposes and probably derive a certain sense of satisfaction from their work. But true joy is found by seeking out God's purpose and then following it, no matter the cost. Joy begins with a surrendered spirit, but it deepens as I actively live a God-purposed life.

Devout believers and nominal churchgoers alike have a deep desire to know God's plan for their lives. Twenty-five million copies of Rick Warren's book attest to that fact. The sticking point for most people, however, is an unwillingness to surrender fully to Christ in the process. We would much prefer a "blueprint only" option—getting a "do-it-yourself kit" from God and then pursuing it in our own way, in our own time, and in our own strength. Like the Crusaders of old, we are keen to pursue our own grandiose dreams and fulfill our own desires—all in God's name. But lasting joy is not found here. A self-purposed life only leads us on a wild-goose chase into familiar territory—the dead-end roads of earthly happiness and personal fulfillment.

How a God-Purposed Life Gives Joy

Writing is a joy for me. More than any other work I can do, I experience a deep sense of delight and satisfaction when I write a book. There's something about crafting a chapter, wordsmithing a paragraph, or tweaking a phrase that completes me in ways impossible to describe. Oh sure, I wrestle and struggle with my manuscript all the time. And occasionally, I am frustrated enough to want to throw it out the window. However, the sting of those struggles is short-lived and only serves to make the joy sweeter when I work through them and finish the project.

I turn once again to the film *Chariots of Fire*, because I think it offers a remarkable portrait of this interrelationship between purpose and joy. The film centers on the true story of Eric Liddell, the Scottish runner-turned-missionary made famous because of his refusal to run on Sunday in the 1924 Summer Olympics. In one scene of the film, Eric shares with his sister why he wants to run in the Olympics before going off to the mission field. He says, "God made me for a purpose — for China. But he also made me fast — and when I run, I feel his pleasure. To give it up would be to hold him in contempt; to win is to honor him."

Eric understood that God's purpose for him would eventually involve going to China as a missionary. But he also recognized that God had something else in store first — *to run like the wind.* And when he lived out that purpose, he experienced God's delight in a way he could not have by doing anything else in the world.

Because of his steadfast faith, Eric would have been joy-filled whether he was a coal miner or an Olympic champion. But what was it specifically about living out his God-given purpose — running — that allowed him to experience a special joy? I see five factors.

Fulfilling God's Unique Design

David has done a variety of jobs in his forty-one years — youth pastor, missionary, part-time college soccer coach, and co-owner of a construction company. However, teaching is what he does best. When I teamed up with him to colead a Sunday school class at our church last year, his teaching gifts were obvious. Whereas I needed to prepare for hours for the discussion, he could wing it and do a much better job than I ever could.

Teaching is not only his gift, but it also is the thing he most loves to do. In fact, he is so convinced of this that he recently gave up a sweetheart job opportunity at a family-owned business. He opted to take the hard road by following God's lead and going back to school for his master's degree.

David's story is not unique inside the church. The apostle Peter tells us that *every* believer receives a gift from Christ and that we should use it to serve one another (1 Peter 4:10). Paul adds that these gifts are distinct and unique to each individual (Rom. 12:6; 1 Cor. 7:7; 12:4–11). Therefore, the purpose of a Christian emerges as the actual living out of the gift that God has given to us.* As I do so, joy happens.

Just as the joy of Jesus Christ was centered on doing what his Father sent him to do, so also his followers experience the same. Oswald Chambers put it like this: "Joy means the perfect fulfillment of that for which I was created and regenerated."

Something about the Work Itself

Doug is a contractor from our church who built our home five years ago. He runs a small home-building business and

---

*A purpose is not necessarily the same as a *calling*. In many cases, the two are identical: I live out my calling as I live out my purpose. But the reality is that we may be called by God to do something that we don't really see as our purpose, even if we are using our apparent gifts.

retains a couple of employees. Doug spends much of his time managing the overall construction projects, but every chance he gets, he loves to work with his hands, particularly the finishing details. I remember coming by our house just a couple of weeks before it was scheduled to be completed. Rather than delegating the job to one of his workers, I found him personally crafting the final woodworking details of the house—making sure the grooves in the beams matched the grooves on the stairway. They were, in fact, small niceties that we didn't even have the budget for, but he insisted be done anyway. Just hearing the enthusiasm in his voice when I talked with him about his work, I could sense that few things in life gave him greater satisfaction.

As Doug's story reveals, the very act of doing work we are called to do can give us joy. When God created Adam and Eve, he designed them from the start to get busy doing things—he placed Adam in the orchard in Eden and charged him with caring and maintaining it (Gen. 2:15). Once Adam and Eve sinned, human work became far more difficult (Gen. 3:17–19). However, even in a fallen world, work continues to be ordained by God.

What's more, the type of work doesn't matter. Whether you are called to be a pastor or a plumber, a singer, or a sanitary worker—all work is equal before God. No purpose is any more significant in God's eyes than another. Protestant Reformer Martin Luther explains:

> To serve God simply means to do what God has commanded and not to do what God has forbidden. And if only we would accustom ourselves properly to this

view, the entire world would be full of service to God, not only the churches but also the home, the kitchen, the cellar, the workshop, and the field of townsfolk and farmers. It is certain that God would have that sort of order not only in the church and world order but also in the home. All, therefore, who serve the latter purpose—father and mother first, then the children, and finally the servants and neighbors—are jointly serving God; for so He wills and commands.

Luther then goes on to show how every believer can receive joy in their work regardless of what they do:

In the light of this view of the matter a poor maid should have the joy in her heart of being able to say: "Now I am cooking, making the bed, sweeping the house. Who has commanded me to do these things? My master and mistress have. Who has given them this authority over me? God has. Very well, then it must be true that I am serving not them alone but also God in heaven and that God must be pleased with my service. How could I possibly be more blessed? Why, my service is equal to cooking for God in heaven!"

In this way a man could be [joyful] and of good cheer in all his trouble and labor; and if he accustomed himself to look at his service and calling in this way nothing would be distasteful to him. But the devil opposes this point of view tooth and nail, to keep one from coming to this joy and to cause everybody to have a special dislike for what he should do and is commanded to do. So the devil operates in order to make sure that people do not love the idea of work and at the same time to rob them of the joy they feel and to diminish their service to God.

When I am doing what God designed me for, I experience a joy that I would not receive if I were doing something else. And the converse is also true. If I do something that is not God's plan for me, I'll end up living an incomplete life. Suppose I traded careers with Doug. I suspect I'd build a house of cards and he'd probably throw my laptop out the window. We would both be miserable. Give me my laptop and give Doug his hammer.

Getting Me out of Myself

When we are living out God's purpose for our lives, we are doing something that gets us beyond ourselves and concerns that we have for our own personal happiness. Take my wife Kimberly. To make ends meet for our household, she works three nights a week as an RN. But if you talk with her, you will quickly discover that homeschooling is her real joy. In spite of the challenges of teaching your own kids, the multitasking hassles, and the frequent exhaustion, she wouldn't have it any other way.

"Joy can be real," Leo Tolstoy wrote, "only if people look upon their life as a service, and have a definite object in life outside themselves and their personal happiness." Kimberly is a living testimony of that biblical truth; as she devotes her energy, creativity, and time to the boys, she is far more focused on them than on her own needs. Christ is then able to let joy overflow in her heart as she carries out this God-given purpose.

Focusing on What Matters

Preaching is a joy for Eric. After walking away from a long career as a high-ranking corporate executive, he is now driven by purpose in the pulpit. He lives in a pressure cooker environment—being the lone pastor of a church bursting at its seams. Yet Eric is constantly refreshed by the combination of studying Scriptures for hours each week and preaching from the pulpit on Sunday mornings.

When we work according to God's purpose, we are working for eternity and for his future kingdom. Some, such as Eric, are gifted in evangelism and preaching. However, God uses us in a variety of ways to accomplish his eternal purposes. Not only can we lead others to God, but we can also help take back the world from Satan and the side effects of sin—such as a doctor battling disease, a Christian artist introducing light into a dark world, a homemaker cleaning the house, and even kids mopping the floors as part of their chores. There is no "busy work" within the body of Christ; it all matters.

Revealing Eternity

We have a creative God, one who created the earth and the skies out of nothing and filled it with boundless diversity and imagination. He invites us to participate in his creative process. John, lead guitarist of the musical group Jordan's Crossing, is an artist who does just that. A highly regarded musician and songwriter, he was heavily involved in the secular music scene for years before his conversion. John's passion for music has spanned his life both as a non-Christian and as a Christian. But while he was driven by music before Christ, he is now driven by Christ to music. "Before I was a believer, I looked to music for enjoyment, money, pride, and personal fulfillment," reflects John. "But today, even my perspective on music has been redeemed. Music is no longer just about the song or the musicianship. Instead, it's about Christ in the music and the music glorifying Christ."

To write a song, pen a novel, or paint a picture that no one has ever conceived of before is a God-breathed activity, designed and ordained by Christ—both for this world and the one to come. In doing so, we give God glory by revealing more of his nature, truth, and creation to others. John sees the relationship between creativity and joy as being clearly evident in the Scriptures. He observes, "Psalm 33, for example, is all about creativity, the skill to execute, and Godly joy. In my case, I am driven by Christ to excellence for him through music. Then, as I edify the church and build Christ up as I perform, the end result is joy."

The Underpurposed Life

In the economic world, the underemployed are persons who work, but their jobs do not make full use of their skills. Along the same lines, some believers live an *underpurposed* life. In their heart, they want to make full use of their gifts, but for a variety of reasons, they're not doing so. The danger lies when this lack of purpose begins to suck the joy out of a believer's heart.*

A significant number of Christians struggle with knowing where they are gifted and how to use these gifts in their lives. Others know exactly what their purpose is and desperately want to live it out, but they are unable to do so. It could simply be a matter of timing. Or perhaps it is something messier, such as a physical limitation or an unexpected obstacle in the way.

The church also contains many who have followed God's purpose for a time, but who have lost the joy that they originally had in what they do. The startling number of pastors who suffer from depression and burnout points to the extent of this problem. Maybe they are exhausted. Maybe they have forgotten their initial vision. They may even question whether what they are doing now is actually God's purpose for them in the first place.

An underpurposed life is a drain on our spiritual life because we so naturally yearn for a purpose and passion to fuel what we do and how we spend our time. Joy stops flowing in us the moment we turn inward and begin to feel underutilized, underappreciated, and undervalued. When we do, we are tempted to wrestle control from God and reclaim our purpose for ourselves.

---

*A God-purposed life may involve our profession, but it certainly need not be the case. A mailman, for example, delivers the mail to pay the bills, but knows his real purpose is for his family to adopt and raise two Chinese orphans. A newly retired schoolteacher clears her schedule so she can direct her church's Sunday school program. An investment banker works on Wall Street, but only so he can use his salary to help finance a Christian elementary school in Haiti.

I am convinced, however, that when you look at Scripture for answers, an underpurposed life is a misnomer. It doesn't actually exist. *No one* who truly seeks God's purpose for his life will, when all is said and done, end up without one. The purpose may not be exactly what we are expecting. And we may experience it in ways wholly different from what we anticipate, plan, or even want. But God never leaves anything underutilized or "on the table," so to speak.

If you find yourself living an underpurposed life, take encouragement from the Old Testament book of Isaiah. When this prophet penned his words to the Israelites, he was writing to a nation going through one of its lowest points in history. The Israelites had lost the original purpose and joy they had during the glory days of Moses, David, and Solomon. They were now a defeated nation. Yet in Isaiah 40, Isaiah turns weariness and joylessness around. He exhorts his people not to remain where they are, but to surrender themselves and call on God for his help:

> *Do you not know?*
> > *Have you not heard?*
> *The LORD is the everlasting God,*
> > *the Creator of the ends of the earth.*
> *He will not grow tired or weary,*
> > *and his understanding no one can fathom.*
> *He gives strength to the weary*
> > *and increases the power of the weak.*
> *Even youths grow tired and weary,*
> > *and young men stumble and fall;*

> *but those who hope in the LORD*
> *will renew their strength.*
> *They will soar on wings like eagles;*
> *they will run and not grow weary,*
> *they will walk and not be faint. (Isa. 40:28–31)*

"Bankable" is a term that Hollywood applies to the top stars in the business, such as Julia Roberts, Tom Hanks, or Johnny Depp. The very presence of a bankable star in a film is enough to guarantee financing for the project as well as assure strong box-office success. That same term is appropriate for Isaiah 40. Isaiah's promise is bankable for the underpurposed, underjoyed believer. God doesn't get tired or weary, and his joy never wears out. As we surrender to him, he reinvigorates and reenergizes us.

To the believer who has lost a sense of purpose, God offers to renew the original passion we once had. To the believer who is searching, he can provide guidance and strength for the search. To the believer who is waiting, he can provide encouragement, hope, and peace even when things don't work out as we expect. But God's promise is only bankable when we get out of the way and allow him to be the focal point—it is *his* purpose for our lives and *his* strength to carry it out.

Keeping the Faith

It has been several years since Mitch and I have had lunch together. I am now living a coast away in New England. Mitch resides in Oregon, and he continues to work as a copier salesman. He remains as convinced as ever that fulltime ministry is

his purpose, sooner or later. However, despite several tantaliz-
ing prospects and near misses, God has not yet opened up an
opportunity for him.

Though driven by a purpose not yet fulfilled, Mitch offers
a model of how to avoid an underpurposed life. He remains
ever joyful as he waits patiently in expectation and anticipation
for what's in store. By leading several ministries at his home
church, he is also using his gifts to the fullest extent that he
can given his situation. Mitch has discovered that there is joy
to be found not only in living a God-purposed life, but also in
the very pursuit of that dream.

Mitch has served an invaluable role in my life as well. He
has been a modern-day Barnabas, a constant encourager, to
me over the past three years. "Keep the faith, do not get discouraged," Mitch wrote to me some time ago in an email. "The
glass is half full; it does not leak. Every sentence is a step closer
to your destiny."

Not long after that email, I found myself clinging to Mitch's
words of encouragement. I was locked in a battle — not just
over my purpose, but for my heart of joy.

CHAPTER 9

JOY BUSTERS

What has happened to all your joy?
—Apostle Paul to the Galatians (Gal. 4:15)

Miss Franny said the problem with people here
is that they forgot how to share their sadness,
but what I think is that people forgot how to share their joy.
—Opal, *Because of Winn Dixie*

Trust or bust. My family and I had been surviving financially for a couple of years since I became a full-time writer. I wasn't sure exactly how; my checks were few and far between. Sometimes it felt as if we must be doing it with smoke and mirrors. But chocking it up to God's provision, we were scraping by.

In the past, my unspoken motto always reflected something that a veteran secret agent would say: "I never walk into a place I don't know how to walk out of." I trusted God with my life (or so I said), but I always had a backup plan ready to go just in case something went wrong. Mixing in solid evangelical words like *responsible, wise,* and *prudent* was all the justification I needed.

But no more. With an almost hilarious joy, I threw away my Plan B and embraced a bold new motto, *Trust or bust*. In so doing, I was experiencing a glorious freedom living on the end of the plank. I modeled my faith walk after great Christian saints of old, particularly nineteenth-century evangelist George Müller and missionary Hudson Taylor.

Müller founded and ran several orphanages. Rather than fundraising or asking for donations, he prayed instead, believing God would provide for their needs. Similarly, Taylor trusted God for his support, remaining steadfast even when that help was long in coming. Time and time again, God always came through for these two men, providing Müller and the orphans with food just moments before a meal or supplying Taylor with money for rent on the day it was due. Since Scripture tells us that God doesn't play favorites, I was convinced that he would do the same for anyone who lived by faith in the mold of Müller and Taylor.

A book project fell through that we were counting on to make ends meet. Up until this time, our checking account was tight, but we managed to stay just above water. However, with several months of work now wasted, we began to fall behind. No problem, I boldly proclaimed. After all, I was faithful and obedient. I was doing everything possible within the sphere of opportunity that God had called me to. For one time in my life, I was convinced that I would remain steadfast in the face of hardship—staying patient, holding out for God, and not fixing the problem myself.

The months dragged on with no relief. We continued to fall further and further into a hole. Questions were scrolling through my head. *Should I put blinders on and simply ignore the problem? Should I seek a short-term solution? Should we sell our house? Or should I put my writing on the back burner and get a real job?* God seemed to be utterly silent to my questions.

Still more time passed with no answers. Our situation finally got to the breaking point. I felt like a Müller who didn't receive bread to feed the orphans or a Taylor who didn't get money to pay his landlord. We had crossed the line from "risky" to "reckless," "patient" to "irresponsible." So, pulling a Plan B out of my hat (using equity on our house), I bought some time and got my family out of the immediate crisis. However, my faith as well as that of my wife was stung by the entire ordeal. In our minds, my initiative rescued us, not God. I felt teased by the amazing prayer stories of Müller and Taylor and wondered what possible relevance those have if God doesn't do the same for us today.

For the first time since I began my writing journey, I lost my joy. The idea of *Trust or bust* now seemed silly. After all, from my perspective, I had trusted God and was busted in the process.

The Gang of Five

Since joy is the nature of God flowing inside of a believer, plain logic alone will tell us that any sin we struggle with is going to stifle our joy. However, even when we avoid obvious sinful behavior, there are harmful attitudes that secretly creep into our spiritual life. Once they take root in our hearts, they become habits, shaping the way we think and react to the world around us. Often lying undetected, these deep-seated attitudes are so subtle that even mature believers fail to recognize them as sin.

There are a handful of attitudes, in particular, that believers need to guard against especially — discouragement, fear, grumbling, guilt, and unforgiveness. These five compose what I call the "joy busters" for their obstructive power to block the joy from flowing through the life of a believer.

There is, I should point out, a difference between the immediate emotions that we experience when something goes wrong and the sustained attitudes that stick with us over time. Suppose, for example, my friend Randy loses his job. Walking out of his office after the layoff, he would naturally have an overwhelming feeling of fear and anxiety. That momentary wave of emotion is far less of an issue for a believer, however, compared to what Randy does once he's had a chance to calm down, pray, and reflect on the situation. Does he trust God or does he fall back on himself? Does he blame God for not preventing the hardship, or does he decide to "count it all joy"? Ultimately, does Randy's crisis draw him closer to Christ or more inward to himself?

When something bad happens in our lives, we will begin by reacting to it emotionally.* But once that initial wave of emotion starts to pass, we have a choice. We can deal with these feelings at the emotional level, give them to God, and move on. Or we can cling to these emotions and allow them to become attitudes that burrow into our hearts.

Since getting married, Kimberly and I have moved around the country often enough to have been active in several dif-

---

*The closer we walk with Christ, the less emotion will rule our lives in a crisis. As we mature, the more we'll be able to respond from the spirit rather than from our gut instinct. Oswald Chambers reminds us, "The surest sign of a mature believer is that they don't get into panics."

ferent evangelical churches—eight, in fact. As I think back to all of the mature believers we've gotten to know and love in these congregations, only a small handful ever had their lives significantly impacted by outward or lifestyle sins. However, I cringe at how many of these same people live holy lives on the outside, but experience little joy in their heart. My cringing is not because I am looking down on them, but because I see how easily one of these joy busters almost busted me.

Discouragement

The best is yet to come, proclaims the Bible over and over. Usually when we talk about Christian hope, we point to our perfect, sinless eternity with Christ. But since God is actively involved in our lives, we have reason to hope in today as well. He promises to guide, protect, provide, and transform us in the here and now. In spite of these promises, however, bad things still happen. Plans are foiled. Expectations are undermined. God often doesn't act like we think he should.

When God didn't noticeably respond to my prayers for help or guidance in my crisis, I became disillusioned. Looking back, I don't think I was questioning God himself or his love or abilities. But I was deeply frustrated with him for leaving me all alone and exposed when I was earnestly trying to live by faith. Even worse, all of my assumptions for over two years seemed to be proven wrong. I felt clueless about going forward. When do I wait on God? And when do I solve the problem myself?

It's healthy to get alone with God, blow off steam, and ask him tough questions. But I went beyond questioning. I felt perfectly justified taking on the role of the righteous victim, and I labeled God as the culprit who disappointed me.

But in spite of my well-reasoned arguments, I eventually came to realize that my discouragement, at its core, was really sin. When it takes root in our heart, discouragement breeds despair, which sucks the life out of our spiritual life. "There's nothing so blocks the spirit as gloom and dependency and downheartedness," adds early church father Seraphim.

Fear, Uncertainty, and Doubt

"Chris Milton will put your Social Security dollars at risk," warned the recorded voice that spoke when I picked up the phone one afternoon. "And if we can't trust him with our Social Security, we can't trust him as our governor." Every election season, political campaigns use "FUD" to sway voters away from the opposing candidate. FUD is a marketing buzzword that stands for Fear, Uncertainty, and Doubt. The term, originating in the business world, describes the cutthroat technique of attracting customers to one company's products by scaring them away from competitors (or frightening voters from a candidate). In much the same way, Satan uses fear, uncertainty, and doubt to stress out believers and drain the joy from our spiritual life.

When I consider the effects of FUD on the life of a believer, I think of Stephen. Stephen was heavily involved in several ministries, was regularly a guest preacher at church, and was always the first to volunteer for outreach programs. When I spoke with him about his evangelism efforts, I could see the joy beaming in his eyes. He had a passion for sharing the good news to people around him. So, when I heard that Stephen was laid off from his long-time job, I kind of expected to see a beacon of faith in the midst of uncertainty, an inspiration to other men at our church caught up in corporate downsizing.

But when I talked with Stephen days later, he was in panic mode. All evidence of his peace and joy was gone. In spite of a generous severance package and a healthy savings account, he was stressed out by the uncertainty of what came next. As time passed, Stephen always seemed more concerned with finding a secure job than examining how God might be trying to use this crisis in his life.

Stephen is not alone. Many of us live in fear and become attracted to the sure things in life. Seeking safety, happiness, and good circumstances, we bolt on God and go into protection mode.

Gloom-and-Doom Grumbling

There are probably few things that grieve God more than having his people characterized as grumblers. The Israelites wandering through the desert grumbled about the leadership of Moses and Aaron and many other problems. The Pharisee leadership constantly "grumbled" and "murmured" about Jesus during his earthly ministry. What's more, parts of the early church were commanded by the apostles Paul and James to stop their grumbling. Even today, this negativism robs many churches and individuals of their joy.

"Grumbling" in the original Greek and Hebrew meant an obstinate, deep-seated complaining. All too often, Christians have a reputation of grumbling at the world around us. We are furious with the evils and immorality of postmodern society. But instead of letting God be the outraged party, we take personal offense. We become God's vigilantes, ready to go "Old Testament" and proclaim God's judgment on the sinners around us. Yet, while we can justify ourselves as simply holding up God's moral order, Christians all too often end up sounding like hate mongers to society around us.

Our negativism doesn't stop there. We squabble with others inside the church. We get hung up on disputable doctrinal matters or petty personal issues that get us offtrack from the overall mission of the church. In my email inbox, I occasionally receive messages from Reggie, a longtime believer and elder in his church, which he sends out to everyone in his address book. What strikes me about his emails are how unabashedly critical they are. The theology in Rick Warren's *Purpose Driven Life* is attacked one day, while Mel Gibson's *The Passion* film is deemed unscriptural the next. I've never seen any emails from Reggie that actually said something positive or encouraging about the ministry that someone else is doing. Reggie seems like a pleasant enough guy when I talk with him in person, but there's a harsh, ungracious side to him that resembles a Pharisee far more than it does Jesus Christ.

Finally, perhaps most common of all, the grumbling in our hearts centers on our own lives. "Man is fond of counting his troubles," Fyodor Dostoevsky said, "but he does not count his joys." Francine attended a Bible study I used to teach. She knew the Scriptures and her theology well, had an answer for most every question, and perhaps thought that the study was too pedestrian for someone of her spiritual caliber. But in all her Christian maturity, she never conveyed any semblance of joy. In fact, she usually sounded miserable. Her outlook on her life, her husband, and her family was always pessimistic. Her grumbling even showed up in her physical appearance. Instead of being a "lump of sunshine," her eyes glared, her mouth frowned, and her shoulders slumped.

Grumbling is a cancer on the body of Christ and sucks the joy out of the individual Christian life. The apostle James couldn't have been more straightforward than what he wrote plainly in James 5:9, "Don't grumble against one another." As James understood, not only does it rob believers of our joy and make us miserable, but it prompts the world around us to write us off. Borrowing from H. L. Mencken's description of a puritan, a Christian can be seen as "a person with the haunting fear that someone, somewhere is happy."

Guilt

Jayne felt dirty and unclean. She was committed to growing her marriage and raising godly kids. However, she was involved in a brief extramarital affair at her workplace. Although she broke off the physical relationship almost immediately, she was broken by the guilt and remorse over the sin she had committed. Jayne knew in her head that Christ forgave her the moment she repented, but she was reluctant to forgive herself. God may have thrown away her sin as far as the east is from the west (Ps. 103:12), but she struggled with clinging to it.

Like Jayne, when we commit a major sin, we can believe that we really should suffer for our wrongs and feel miserable. In that light, the idea of experiencing joy becomes unthinkable and something we don't deserve. "The offender never forgives," goes the Russian proverb.

Turning us inward rather than upward, guilt is distinct from what the apostle Paul calls "godly sorrow." Godly sorrow convicts us, but then vanishes as soon as we repent. Guilt hangs around and doesn't go away. Paul contrasts the two in 2 Corinthians 7:10: "Godly sorrow brings repentance that leads to salvation and leaves no regret, but worldly sorrow brings death." In other words, godly sorrow delivers joy, while guilt sucks it away.

Unforgiveness

When a wrong has been committed, guilt can plague the offender. But just as dangerous, unforgiveness can wreak havoc on the spiritual life of the person wronged. John, an acquaintance of mine, was a longtime member of his home church. He had a jovial, lively personality that people enjoyed. But when John's family was the victim of gossip among others in the congregation, he abruptly left the church. In a conversation with him about the situation much later, he claimed to be over the hurt, but I could sense a bitter residue still on his heart. John no longer had the joy that I saw visibly demonstrated in his life before. His hurt had soured his joy.

iLove

Discouragement, fear, grumbling, guilt, and unforgiveness may be triggered by a variety of different conditions, but there is an underlying factor that transforms mere emotion into hardened attitude—a preoccupation with self. When I insist on having things my own way, I stress out when things are uncertain; I get discouraged when things go badly; and I grumble when problems arise. I am experiencing, to borrow a term from Oswald Chambers, "disenchanted self-love."

Both unforgiveness and guilt have direct ties back to the self as well. When I have an unforgiving heart, I refuse to let go of the injustice committed against me, demanding that the wrongs be righted. I may agree intellectually with the need to forgive others just as Christ forgave me, but my heart refuses. The idea of letting go becomes a bitter pill to swallow. Francis de Sales puts it like this: "Self love always magnifies our injuries." The other side of the fence is not much different. When I am wracked by guilt and show an unwillingness to accept God's grace, I am really just claiming part of myself (my past wrongs) and refusing to let God have it.

In his classic *The Great Divorce*, C. S. Lewis shows how a self-centered attitude can harden a heart over a lifetime and make it impossible to experience joy. Lewis tells a story of a group of people living in hell who take a bus trip to heaven. The dozen citizens of hell who are profiled have unique and idiosyncratic personalities, but they all have two common traits. First, they all lacked joy in their earthly life as well as in their life in hell. Second, they are unable to get out of themselves. They were so preoccupied with their own interests and concerns that they would rather go back to hell than surrender them and stay in heaven.

A grumbling lady, for example, talks in a nonstop monologue, complaining about every aspect of her life on earth. The question, one observer from heaven wonders, is whether the lady is "a grumbler, or only a grumble." In other words, the more we allow these sinful attitudes to penetrate our hearts, the more they dehumanize us. We become less and less like Christ and more like a "thing."

A self-conscious woman further shows the effects of being preoccupied with self. She is constantly obsessed with what others think of her and what she looks like. Inhabitants of heaven offer her a chance to stay and enjoy the joys of heaven. For a moment, she genuinely thinks about taking the risk, but in the end, she is too self-conscious about her ghostlike appearance to do so. "Could you, only for a moment, fix your mind on something not yourself?" says an inhabitant of heaven to the lady.

Changes

Changing conduct is far easier than changing a hardened attitude. Bad behavior can be stopped by following Paul's advice to "flee the evil desires of youth" (2 Tim. 2:22). But attitudes burrowed deep in my heart can't be run away from. They have to be dealt with one day at a time. Even tougher, they require that I give up something I hold near and dear to my heart—be it my expectations, my control, my rights, or my righteous stand.

The discouragement I recently faced may not have been a chronic, long-term battle, but it did last long enough to knock the breath out of my spiritual life. As time passed, however, I became convinced that I couldn't let myself continue down this joyless path. Perhaps more than anything else, I was motivated by a brief passage in C. S. Lewis's *Screwtape Letters*, in which a senior devil named Screwtape talks about a believer's perseverance from Satan's perspective:

> Our cause is never more in danger than when a human, no longer desiring, but still intending, to do [God's] will, looks round upon a universe from which every trace of Him seems to have vanished, and asks why he has been forsaken, and still obeys.

Screwtape describes exactly the kind of disciple I wanted to be. I decided I would continue to live by faith even though I was no longer really sure what it meant to live by faith. I would continue to seek God when I wasn't sure I even wanted to. Perhaps I was merely going through the motions at the outset, but over time, an amazing thing began to happen: my heart actually started to change. I slowly and gradually began to take my eyes off myself and my stubborn claims and put them back onto God. And, to my delight, joy returned, even though issues remained that I needed to work through.

Scripture paints a consistent picture that the joy we experience grows as we focus more on who God is and on his love for us. When we know of God's salvation, we can echo the words of the psalmist, "My lips will shout for joy when I sing praise to you—I, whom you have redeemed" (Ps. 71:23). When we know of God's mercy, we will join in saying, "I will be glad and rejoice in your love, for you saw my affliction and knew the anguish of my soul" (Ps. 31:7). When we learn of his faithfulness, we exclaim, "Sing joyfully to the LORD, you righteous ... he is faithful in all he does" (Ps. 33:1–4). When we know of God's truth, we cry out, "I rejoice in your promise like one who finds great spoil" (Ps. 119:162).

The restoration in my spiritual life had begun. Not that my rediscovered joy was going to go unchallenged, however. There would soon be threats by something approaching me in the rearview mirror.

CHAPTER 10

GLORY DAYS

Remember Lot's wife! Whoever tries to keep his life will lose it,
and whoever loses his life will preserve it.

—Luke 17:32–33

Holy Lot was a-going behind God's angel,
He seemed huge and bright on a hill, huge and black.
But the heart of his wife whispered stronger and stranger:
"It's not very late, you have time to look back
At these rose turrets of your native Sodom,
The square where you sang, and the yard where you span,
The windows looking from your cozy home
Where you bore children for your dear man."
She looked—and her eyes were instantly bound
By pain—they couldn't see any more at all:
Her fleet feet grew into the stony ground,
Her body turned into a pillar of salt.

—Anna Akhmatova, "Lot's Wife," Russia, 1923

I peaked a decade ago, at least according to my résumé. In the
years following my rise up the corporate ladder in Silicon Valley and subsequent departure from the high tech world, Jesus

Christ has blessed me with several great opportunities in the field of writing. But, as I've shared, times are still tough and answers are often slow to come. At moments like these, I can find myself listening to the whispers of my past—longing once again to feel important and indispensable. I can find myself looking for joy in the rearview mirror.

God does want me to *remember* what he's done for me in the past; he just doesn't want me to constantly *relive* it. For the moment I start living there, past-tense living sucks the joy out of me and spits out a shell of what I once was. Consider the lives of three individuals who demonstrate these life-draining effects.

Living on the Flip Side

Never give up on the little guy. That message rang in my ears as I watched *Seabiscuit*. This film tells the true-life story of a race horse called Seabiscuit, a trainer named Tom Smith, and a jockey named Red Pollard, each of whom were deemed outcasts in the world of horse racing in the 1930s. Seabiscuit came from a legendary bloodline, but he was considered lazy and was sold at a bargain basement price. Tom was a maverick trainer whose unorthodox methods were scoffed at by the racing community, a relic from the Old West who needed to be put out to pasture. Red was a jockey with enough God-given talent to be a top rider. But his oversized frame, years of neglect, and squandered opportunities left him an also-ran.

The film chronicles how this trio of misfits was brought together and resurrected by Charles Howard, a never-say-die millionaire who believed in second chances. Howard's gamble paid off as Seabiscuit rapidly rose to the pinnacle of horse racing and defeated War Admiral, the most celebrated horse of that era, in a head-to-head match race. In doing so, Seabiscuit emerged as one of the enduring horse-racing legends of all time. As the credits rolled after watching the movie, I was beaming. The final frames of the film depict pure bliss and total satisfaction. Surely they must have all lived happily ever after!

But real life, as I am finding out, isn't always so neat and tidy. These "little guys" may have never given up, but they were never able to match their successes again. In fact, after Seabiscuit's retirement, Tom and Red traveled on separate, lonely roads that descended into obscurity. They lived the rest of their days on the flip side of success.

Tom stayed on for a few more years with Charles, but a nagging back injury forced Charles eventually to replace his aging trainer. Though in his seventies, Tom found a job training another ranking horse. But when one of his stall workers was caught giving the horse a banned substance, Tom was held responsible. In spite of the fact there was not a shred of evidence that he had any knowledge of the incident, Tom was banned for racing for one year. He was never the same after that incident. Even after his suspension was over, his reputation was permanently tarnished, leaving Tom embittered for the rest of his life.

The injury-riddled Red knew it was time to retire after Seabiscuit did, and so he tried his hand at becoming a stable trainer for Charles. It didn't take. Not knowing what else to do, Red decided to turn back the clock and return to the saddle once again. But instead of glory, Red only found humiliation.

He rode bush league horses at second-rate tracks against jockeys who were half his age. Red struggled through one serious injury after another as he watched his riding skills diminish before his eyes. When his body finally gave out in his mid-forties, Red took on various odds jobs, including a mail sorter, a valet, and a lowly boot cleaner for other jockeys. He eventually turned to alcohol, perhaps as a way to escape life on the flip side.

Yesterday's Golden Girl

Veronica Lake was a golden girl in the golden age of movies. The beautiful blonde went from a nobody to a major celebrity within two years. After starring in *I Wanted Wings* in 1941, the public warmly embraced Veronica, and her peek-a-boo bang hairstyle became all the rage in the early 1940s. During a three-year span, she was star of several blockbusters, named twice by *Life* as the top actress of the year, and won a US Army poll for the most popular actress during World War II. But just as quickly as she rose to the top, Veronica's career spiraled downward after a string of mediocre films. By 1948, she was unceremoniously dumped by Paramount Studios.

Now on the underbelly of her career, she made several attempts to recreate her past success off and on during the 1950s and 1960s. She had some minor successes on stage and TV, but nothing lasted. During this time, she fought mental illness and alcoholism and descended into a world far removed from her Hollywood golden years, living in an old, rundown hotel in New York City and working as a barmaid. She died a lonely death a few years later at age fifty-three.

Whispers

When I consider the past-tense lives that Tom, Red, and Veronica led after their falls from success, I am reminded of an obscure character in the Bible, Lot's wife. Not much is known about this Old Testament female — in fact, her name is not even given in the Scriptures.

We do know a little more about her husband. Lot was the nephew of Abraham and, although he should not be confused with being a spiritual giant like his uncle, he was a man of faith. After parting company with Abraham, Lot settled his family in the city of Sodom. Lot and his family lived many joyful years there until God brought judgment on the city (see Gen. 19). But before raining down burning sulfur on the city, God sent two angels to warn Lot. The angels left him with a simple, strict warning: "Don't look back and don't stop anywhere in the plain." So Lot took his wife and daughters and together they fled the city.

If all had gone according to plan, we would have little reason to dwell on Lot's wife today. But she is notorious because of the bad decision she made as she was just outside the city. The Bible provides an exceedingly brief account of the event: *Lot's wife looked back, and she became a pillar of salt.*

My instant response to her decision is to shake my head in disgust. After all, she had but a single, unambiguous command from the Lord to follow — *don't look back*. How could she screw that up? Yet when I read the summary in Genesis, I gloss over the inner turmoil that she must have had raging inside of her. What's more, if I am honest with myself, I have to admit that what went on within her probably looks a lot like the debates that go on in my heart as well.

I can envision Lot's wife running alongside her husband as they race beyond the outskirts of the city. Yet the further they go, reluctance builds. She starts to slowly let up on her pace while Lot moves ahead, unaware of his wife's growing hesitation. Just steps ahead of her two daughters now, she starts to hear the whispers of her heart—the hometown in which she raised her family, the house she worked so hard to decorate, the evening dinners with dear friends, and the comfort and safety of a place she knew so well. As tears roll down her cheeks, Lot's wife stops in her tracks. Sodom is all she knows; how could she be expected to just leave it behind? Her husband and daughters race on ahead, while she goes beyond the point of no return. Ignoring God's command, she turns her head.

Lot's wife is the poster child for past-tense living. In a real way, her salty fate describes exactly what happened to Tom, Red, and Veronica. These three may not have been transformed into statues of sodium chloride, but they lived out the remainder of their days just as if they had. Their lives drifted away piece by piece because they were unable to turn their hearts around and live in the present.

As far as I can tell, Tom, Red, and Veronica were not believers and so never had God's joy living inside of them. Regardless, these stories still frighten me because I believe I could easily be transformed into a salt pillar like them. I too have had past experiences that brought profound joy, meaning, and significance to my life. What's stopping them from chasing me down and haunting me?

Consequences

Perhaps I should give Tom, Red, and Veronica a break. Maybe past-tense living is understandable for non-Christians. After all, if people have no hope in the future, then clinging to the past is all they have. Not so for believers. As C. S. Lewis points out after reflecting on Dante's classic *Inferno*, "Notice that in Dante the lost souls are entirely concerned with their past. Not so the saved ... We must try very hard not to keep on endlessly chewing the cud."

As a result, the more I understand who God is and how he works, the more I realize that I cannot experience joy when I am holding onto the past. Jesus makes this point clear when he speaks to his disciples about being ready for his second coming. Indeed, Jesus uses Lot's wife as a prime example of what not do to. "Remember Lot's wife!" he teaches in Luke 17:32–33. "Whoever tries to keep their life will lose it, and whoever loses their life will preserve it." Out of the many people in the Old Testament who made lousy decisions, I am intrigued that Jesus singled her out. Clearly Lot's wife offers a case study for how a believer must not live.

Utterly Useless

When I live in the past, I discover I am utterly useless to God in the present. Like Lot's wife stopping and turning the other way, I am no longer moving forward in obedience to Jesus Christ. God's will, in effect, leaves me behind, and I become as useful to God as a salt pillar in the dusty plains of the Jordan.

Jesus Christ is able to use his disciples only when they die to themselves, take up their cross, and follow him. Consider, for example, the disciple wannabe in Matthew 8, who said he would like to follow Jesus but first needed to go bury his father. Jesus responded, "Follow me, and let the dead bury their own dead" (v. 22). Jesus, in effect, is telling the man to stop dragging his feet if he wants to follow him. As with this disciple, excuses will not cut it for me either; the ministry of Jesus will simply go on without me.

Out of Synch

Past-tense living gets me out of synch with God and resistant to how he operates. God does not do encores. Once he's done something, he moves on and doesn't look back. However, my human nature constantly fools me into thinking he just might bring back the glory days. Perhaps he will get a cookie cutter out and recreate another situation like the one I once had. I find myself sounding like Lucy in C. S. Lewis's *Prince Caspian*. In an exchange between Lucy and Aslan, the Christ-like figure of the story, she expresses her disappointment:

> I was so pleased at finding you again. [But] I thought you'd come roaring in and frighten all the enemies away—like last time. And now everything is spoiled.

Aslan is quick to remind Lucy, much to her chagrin, that things never happen the same way twice. Christians are equally susceptible to overlooking that truth. Consider, for example, my father, who is a missionary serving West Africa.

Back in the 1980s, their mission in Liberia was thriving. They had numerous missionaries working in a village called Ganta that ministered to hundreds of people through a hospital and Christian school. Each of the missionaries who served there can joyfully recount a multitude of stories of God's amazing work at the mission.

However, civil war erupted in Liberia over a decade ago and destroyed most of the mission's buildings and infrastructure. Now that the fighting has died down, many of these same missionaries want to rebuild the station just like it was in the 1980s. But if these missionaries are not looking to Jesus Christ, they can easily find themselves trying to recreate the past. Instead of being directed forward by God, they can be preoccupied with their former success. What's more, they can even become a stumbling block to their ministry if they grow resistant to new ideas that God may be trying to engineer in this new situation.

Before I left for Silicon Valley, I led the best Bible study group I've ever been a part of. The group attended week in and week out, loved to debate and discuss the lesson for hours, and were vulnerable and open with each other. In fact, leaving that group was the single hardest part of the decision to move to California. So when we returned to New England years later, I was thrilled at the prospect of resurrecting the group study once again. It was never quite the same. God had more blessings in store, but for a long while, I was only looking for a reunion tour.

Misdirected Security and Identity

When I live in the past, I find my security and identity going back rather than in the "uncertain certainty" of God's present.

Past-tense living requires no trust in God. I already know the ending, how it all plays out. I also have an identity and self-worth when I look back at good times. *That's when life was good, when life had meaning,* I say to myself. But in doing so, I lack faith that God can bring about joyful days in the future.

During their journey from Egypt to the Promised Land, the Israelites fell into this trap. When the Pharaoh's army threatened them before the crossing of the Red Sea, many began to wish they had never left in the first place. Later, when times got rough as the Israelites wandered through the desert for forty years, they once again became nostalgic for—of all places—Egypt. In spite of the fact that they had been enslaved by Pharaoh and forced to work hard labor, the Israelites started to look for security and stability by looking back. The idea of having a reliable source of food rather than trusting in God for daily provision appealed to them. As a result, they complained and whined about returning to the "good ol' days" of bondage and slavery.

When I have my eyes focused ahead, I will constantly be stretched by Jesus Christ to discover new joy. While Tom, Red, Veronica, and Lot's wife could not see their present apart from the past, the clear message of Jesus in Luke 17—*Remember Lot's wife*—is that his disciples are required to. God wants us to live in his "uncertain certainty" in the present. And when we do so, Dietrich Bonhoeffer points out the irony between a past mistakenly thought secure and a present where the true security lies:

> The disciple is dragged out of his relative security
> into a life of absolute insecurity (that is, in truth, into the

absolute security and safety of the fellowship of Jesus), from a life which is observable and calculable (it is, in fact, quite incalculable) into a life where everything is unobservable and fortuitous (that is, into one which is necessary and calculable), out of the realm of finite (which is in truth the infinite) into the realm of infinite possibilities (which is the one liberating reality).

In other words, the only time we are truly secure and have an identity is when we give up the reins to our lives, including our past, and simply trust in him alone.

Deadening

When I choose to live in the past, I deaden my spirit. Tom, Red, and Veronica reached mountaintops in their lives, but they could never move on. And when they could not get back to those peaks, they became lifeless. Tom tried to recreate success but grew embittered by his failed attempts. Red hung on to the reins of horses as long as he possibly could. And when his body would not hang on anymore, he turned to alcohol as a substitute. Veronica spent her days living in the past, and like Red, turned to the bottle when Hollywood passed her by. Past-tense living causes us to waste away and then to look for substitutes when we cannot find the joy for which we are so desperately looking.

Echoes of Something Greater

The nineteenth-century English poet William Wordsworth was a romantic. The focus of much of his poetry is on remembrance of things past. He believed that if he could just get back to those times, he'd find the joy he craved. His early memories were not even all that peaceful, yet they still grabbed hold of his heart, and his best poetry was a set of poems that reflected those emotions.

Like Wordsworth, I too am a dyed-in-the-wool romantic, and I have a tendency to idealize experiences in the past and make them better than they really were. In the words of Owen Barfield, a past experience for me becomes "a whisper which memory will warehouse as a shot." I think of my college days, in which my only responsibilities were to study, get good grades, and eat pizza. Or the God-ordained purpose I felt when a friend and I rode our bikes across the country to raise thousands of dollars for a mission project in Haiti. Or the adventure of my early marriage when we moved to various parts of the country before settling down.

These experiences were not overly blissful at the time. In fact, they were often downright difficult. But as the years go by, those past experiences begin to acquire an almost mythical quality. When times get tough in the present, I find myself longing for the return of the past. I convince myself that's where the joy is.

Yet when I dwell on the past and find an unbalanced meaning in my experiences, I mistake the past for what it really was. Those things that I seek in the past are only longings of something else, traces of what God has in store for me in eternity: joy. The pleasures of the past, according to C. S. Lewis, are meant to point the way to God, just as making love is a forerunner that leads to something even greater — a child of your own—or as the honeymoon is but a precursor to a lifetime with your dearest love.

As I wrestle with living joy, I am beginning to see that God is able to do much more than simply put Band-Aids over my lack of faith, skewed attitudes, and longings for the past. Far more significantly, he transforms our greatest struggles into the greatest opportunities we can have on this earth—in order to experience Jesus Christ's lasting joy. God brought three people into my life who helped me understand the power of this truth.

CHAPTER 11

PROVING GROUNDS

One sees great things from the valley;
only small things from the peak.
—G. K. Chesterton

[God] seems to need these darker hours,
these empty-hearted hours, to mean the most to people.
—Frank Laubach

"Count it all joy!" I shouted to my wife in a desperate attempt to find some humor in the situation. Moments before, my laptop had crashed as I was working on the manuscript of this book. It was just the latest in a series of mishaps and problems that had plagued us over the spring. The death of my laptop was inconvenient and expensive, but I remained calm and upbeat. I smiled in the face of adversity — *just like Indiana Jones*, I said to myself. However, in the back of my mind, I wondered whether I'd really be able to shrug off more serious troubles with a simple "count it all joy."

The apostle James, in the opening sentences of his letter, instructs us to "consider it pure joy ... when you face trials of many kinds" (James 1:2). The New English Bible translates the phrase as "consider it *nothing but joy*" (italics added). James is not suggesting that we should sprinkle joy onto a tough situation to somehow make it seem sweeter. Instead, we are to experience joy in all its fullness as we face trials. The idea that we as believers can actually be joyful in the worst moments of our lives is a remarkable promise of Scripture. But the problem is that the claim has a pie-in-the-sky quality that makes it easy to dismiss. It is reduced to being little more than the Christian equivalent of *hakuna matata* ("no worries").

As I reflect on the words of James, I can't avoid the high bar he sets for God's gift of joy. Any lingering confusion between joy and happiness must end with this passage. If I claim to be happy when my life has been turned upside down, I am either lying or deluding myself, or I am downright insane. Happiness and trouble simply don't mix. But according to James, I can rejoice in the same situation. If he is correct, then God's joy must be made up of material so strong and sturdy that it can withstand the toughest pain and sorrow that this world can thrust upon us. Trials thus emerge as joy's greatest and toughest proving grounds.

I can talk till I am blue in the face about having this sort of joy in the midst of a laptop crash and financial struggles. But what about believers who face hardships that make my problems look trivial by comparison? Can they, like James and Peter claim, rejoice? Or when difficulties come, does joy prove just as flighty as happiness?

Overjoyed by Trial

Everybody at Heritage Bible Chapel knows Judy. She's the ambassador of joy, the bubbly woman who always seeks out visitors and makes them feel right at home. She is a "need meeter," possessing a heart that rejoices most when she is able to help others.

Judy's joy was put on trial, however, with a phone call from her doctor three years ago. She was scheduled for a follow-up appointment the next day to discuss the results of an examination. However, when the doctor discovered that Judy had a cancerous tumor, he phoned her immediately. The early call, the doctor said, would give her time to get over the initial shock before they met in his office to discuss treatment.

Judy may have faced many difficulties in her life, but she was still astonished by the news. Only in her early sixties, she wasn't ready to deal with these sorts of life-and-death issues just yet. Any panic and fright that flooded her mind that evening was short-lived, however. She received a call from a close friend soon after who encouraged her with a simple phrase, "It's not about you. It is about him." Those words would become Judy's mantra throughout her entire treatment period.

Judy knelt down to pray after she got off the phone. As she did so, she began to turn everything over to God—the uncertainty of what came next, the anxiety over the chemotherapy, the fear of dying. The burden of the ordeal became lighter and lighter as she surrendered each issue and concern to God. When the prayer was over, she sensed a sudden change in her spirit; an indescribable peace and joy flooded her heart. As Judy reflects on that prayer today, she sees it as the pivotal turning point before the treatment even started. From that point on, Judy sailed through the next several months, never once taking on her sickness for herself.

Not that everything went smoothly. When Judy began her chemotherapy, unexpected complications arose that stretched her faith even further. First, she discovered that during the course of her treatments, she could not take the arthritis medicine she depended on. If her arthritis flared up, she'd have to cope with severe pain and not be able to do anything about it. Second, just a month into the treatment, Judy was informed that her landlord was selling the apartment that she was living in. She had to quickly find a suitable replacement, pack, and move—the last thing she wanted to deal with given her present physical state.

In spite of these frustrations, Judy was doing far more than just trying to survive the ordeal. She was living through it with a dynamic, contagious joy. Judy saw the entire experience as an opportunity to live out Christ's command in Matthew 5:40, to "let [her] light shine." From her doctor to the nurses, the technicians, and office secretary, everybody was amazed by her joyous outlook. As a result, she stumbled into opportunities to share her faith on an almost daily basis.

Over her entire life, Judy always had a heart for serving other people. Yet as she looks back, she realizes that many of those acts of service were done with good intentions, but under her own power. Because of her cancer, God was able to shape and mold Judy to begin to serve on his strength, not hers. With a sparkle in her eyes, Judy will tell you today that she knows the key to lasting joy: "It's not about me. It's about him."

Alone with God

A fairy-tale marriage, a blessed life. Linda always had every-thing that she could ever ask for. She was married to Bob, a successful businessman and a man of faith and character. The two of them were an attractive, fun-loving couple, possessing an engaging charm that made you want to hang around them. Bob and Linda had three boys who were healthy and well adjusted and who shared their parents' faith.

They became active in a new church thirty miles from their home. In fact, they were so committed to the church and to their Christian friends that they decided to move farther away from Bob's workplace in order to live nearby the church. As Linda moved into her beautiful new house, the rural New England setting was idyllic, a heaven on earth they hoped would last for decades to come.

Her storybook life took a tragic twist just a few months later with an ominous knock on her front door. It was a chilly March morning, and Linda opened the door to find a grim-faced state trooper with news to share. Sitting Linda down, the trooper relayed the events of the morning. On his way to the airport, Bob was involved in an automobile accident, and the report was not good. In an effort to dodge a swerving car, Bob's automobile had veered off of the highway and struck a tree. Bob, the trooper explained, had been killed instantly from the impact. He was just forty-three years old.

Linda had been a believer for many years, but her life was so charmed that, in her own words, she never really needed God. After all, Bob or her tight-knit family had always met any kind of need she had. But from that day on, God began to take over that space in her heart that other people had always occupied.

Molding a heart is a gradual, patient process for the Lord. His first step was simply to give Linda the strength and courage to make it through the funeral and immediate days that followed. Then, as the weeks went by, Linda found herself in escape mode—doing everything she could to avoid the heartbreak of being all alone. She kept her schedule as busy as possible and had a constant stream of visitors in her home.

But as time passed, God gently tugged on her heart. In response, Linda gradually gave up her claim to Bob and her fairy-tale life. And in doing so, she began experiencing an intimacy with Christ incomparable to anything she knew before the accident. As she recollects all that has happened, she can point to the exact moment that she experienced joy in the aftermath of Bob's passing—the first time in which she could be alone with God and be content with him.

Joy on a Ventilator

Donovan speaks slowly and methodically as he lies in his bed at Wachusett Extended Care Facility. Normal speech is impossible for the fifty-three-year-old quadriplegic, since he can only enunciate words when he exhales through his ventilator. Words may come slow when you talk with him, but the joy that radiates from this native-born Jamaican flies at you at light speed.

Donovan was paralyzed from the neck down after he was involved in a car accident in 1984. At the time, his passion in life was his brand new Pontiac Trans Am. In fact, he took a second job just so he could afford the car payment. But his burning of the candle at both ends proved to be his undoing. As he raced from one job to the next, he lost control of his vehicle, hit a tree, and was thrown out through the T-roof, landing on his head. Donovan suffered a C-three spinal fracture, though doctors expressed amazement that Donovan wasn't killed from the crash.

Donovan had made a confession of faith as a teenager in Jamaica, but had fallen far away from Christ as he got older and settled in the United States. As he reflects on the accident now, he views it as God's wake-up call to him. Pain, as C. S. Lewis once said, is God's megaphone. Not long after arriving at the hospital, Donovan listened loud and clear to this overpowering voice. He realized that everything he'd been living for since his youth was so easily taken away. He wanted no more of that dead-end living. Though his legs no longer worked, he imagined himself running to the open arms of his heavenly Father.

Much of Donovan's life since his paralysis has been characterized by a series of disappointments, setbacks, and shattered dreams. His newlywed wife initially tried to play the supportive spouse, but it didn't take; she soon left him and filed for divorce. His physical condition never improved. Initial hopes of recovering some movement in his limbs proved groundless. His many attempts even to breathe on his own were also unsuccessful. Donovan eventually had to resign himself to living the rest of his life on a ventilator.

To make matters worse, Donovan has never been able to live independently outside of a hospital environment. For several years, he worked desperately on the logistics to get approval for state assistance, arrange for round-the-clock care, find a roommate willing to help in night hours, and locate an appropriate apartment. Twice he came tantalizingly close to actually pulling it off. But it was not to be; something always came up blocking his plans. He was eventually forced to give up on this dream altogether.

In spite of many defeats and constant feelings of helplessness, his joy-filled spirit has allowed him to overcome these trials. Even in the early months following the accident, Donovan could find joy in the simplest of events. A sun ray shining over his body on a cold November morning. A new roommate who could communicate with him verbally and help keep him company. Getting dressed up and going outdoors for an afternoon.

More than anything else, however, Donovan has been fueled by his hope in Christ. He can almost taste what's next: an eternity with his Savior, sporting a new body with legs for running, a pair of arms for hugging, a set of lungs that breathe on their own, and a mouth that is free to speak, shout, and sing.

Over the years, he has occasionally struggled with bouts of discouragement and bitterness. But at the end of each of these tests, his faith and joy prove genuine as he utters the words of Job, "Though he slay me, yet will I hope in him" (Job 13:15).

Raiders of the Lost Joy

During my research, I came across a best-selling evangelical Bible study concluding that, based on James 1:2, the appropriate response for a believer when trials come is to (1) immediately give thanks to God and (2) take on a joyful attitude.

Oh really? Had the author penned those words from actual experience? Not satisfied, I turned to the Phillips paraphrase of the New Testament and read the same passage. It said, "Don't resent [trials] as intruders, but welcome them as friends." I then checked out the popular paraphrase *The Message*, which puts it like this: "Consider it a sheer gift."

Welcome as friends? Treat like a birthday gift? These interpretations seem so canned and superficial in comparison to the raw kind of joy I have seen displayed in the lives of Judy, Linda, and Donovan. When my friend Dan gets laid off, is he supposed to "immediately give thanks"? Is Mark supposed to welcome his cancer and painful chemotherapy treatments as "friends"? In order to be obedient, is my neighbor Karen called to instantly "take on a joyful attitude" when her husband suddenly walks out on her? Surely this is not what James meant when we are told to "consider it pure joy"!

This superficial understanding of the apostle's teaching is what I would call "Indy joy"—an Indiana Jones version of the real thing. It's a smirk in the face of disaster—a gritty determination to persevere no matter the odds. Donning a fedora and a leather jacket, we memorize James 1:2 and become bent on being joyful in a crisis. Then, in true Indiana Jones fashion, when the tidal wave comes our way, we resourcefully grab a life raft and attempt to ride out the storm.

The fundamental problem with Indy Joy is that it becomes something attained by willpower alone. By sheer strength of character, we can force ourselves to do amazing things under stress. The cinemas are full of these kinds of heroic tales. But Indy Joy is no epic; it has a shorter running time than most children's animated films. I can psyche myself up, give out the high fives, and pack a smile for a little while. But once I begin to actually deal with pain and suffering, then the paper-thin joy I had fades away.

No matter how resolved I am, I can't *will* joy. It just doesn't work that way. I can *choose* joy as I surrender my claim to myself, but I cannot will a joyful attitude. In the end, a smile in the face of danger makes for a good close-up shot of Harrison Ford, but it doesn't draw me any closer to Jesus Christ.

Christians have a long history of showing steadfast faith in the face of certain disaster. Take the early church leader Polycarp as an example. Authoritative accounts depict him as a man filled with courage and joy in the moments leading up to his execution, utterly astounding his Roman executioners. I don't think Polycarp was trying to pull an Indiana Jones here. Rather, fueled by the certainty of his faith, he remained calm in spite of the physical pain he would soon be facing. However, suppose Polycarp was forced to watch his wife and children be tortured and executed instead. He may have been just as courageous and certain about their future glory, but I don't think he would, to quote that popular Bible study again, "immediately take on a joyful attitude."

Mixing Joy and Grief

The apostles plainly tell us that hard times are inevitable, designed to test our faith, strengthen our endurance, and conform us into the image of Christ. As Peter says, trials come so that a believer's faith may be proved authentic (1 Peter 1:7). "Pain plants the flag of truth within a rebel fortress," is how C. S. Lewis describes it. In other words, when our lives resemble a

Life Is Good T-shirt, our faith can mature—but only to a certain level. Comfort and happiness form a glass ceiling that prevent us from furthering our intimacy with God. As Linda's story demonstrates, only when our faith is stretched to the breaking point and we are truly at the end of ourselves are we apt to release everything into the arms of Jesus Christ.

Seen in this light, joy in times of hardship no longer seems pie-in-the-sky at all, but starts to make perfect sense. Trials are meant to bring us to the point of surrender. And surrender, as I discussed earlier in the book, is the key to opening the floodgates of joy in our lives. Our willingness to give everything over to God during times of sorrow and distress is precisely why joy is so capable of shining through.

Happiness and sorrow are mutually exclusive, but joy and grief walk hand in hand. Peter tells us that the two naturally coexist in the life of a believer—we can rejoice greatly as we grieve greatly in all kinds of trials (1 Peter 1:6).

Even Jesus Christ—the perfect "man of joy"—experienced sorrow. The prophet Isaiah refers to Jesus as a "man of sorrows" (Isa. 53:3 NIV). Even more telling is the account of Lazarus in John 11. When his friend Lazarus died, Jesus didn't offer condolences to Lazarus's sister Mary, tell her to give thanks, and explain that his death was God's will. Instead, he was heartbroken by the event. The gospel of John packages it ever so succinctly in the Bible's shortest verse: "Jesus wept" (John 11:35). As Jesus Christ shows us, there are certain trials that we will experience in this broken world in which mourning and heartache are going to take center stage—for a time.

Joy resides deep inside a surrendered heart and stays burrowed there, even when the flood waters of emotional strife
sweep through. Joy doesn't flee pain but mixes freely with it.
But not stopping there, joy also provides solid footing for us
to stand on as emotions rise and fall like roaring waves. Over
time, as the emotional waters begin to subside, the joy that was
constant throughout starts to become manifest once again.

The gospel of Matthew talks at length about the agony Jesus
faced in the Garden of Gethsemane the night before his crucifixion. Judas had already left during the supper earlier in order
to betray him, and Jesus knew that the soldiers would soon be
coming after him. He prayed three times to be spared from the
cross, agonizing over the separation from his Father that would
occur in a few short hours. His closest disciples fell asleep in
his hour of greatest need and would shortly after desert him.
Yet in spite of his suffering, the book of Hebrews tells us, "For
the joy set before him [Jesus] endured the cross, scorning its
shame" (Heb. 12:2). In other words, the joy of Jesus Christ
never wavered or faltered even as he went through those hor-
rific final hours.

We too can emulate Christ's joy as we endure in a trial.
However, like Jesus in the Garden of Gethsemane, this joy is
not something that is always noticeable in the darkest of days,
except in the delight that comes from intimacy with our heavenly Father. Judy, Linda, and Donovan all observe that God's
ever-present joy is sometimes best understood in the rearview
mirror, looking back and seeing how much was accomplished
by him through the situation.

The Joy Alternative

In the past, I tended to dismiss James 1:2 as an ideal to aspire to, something akin to Jesus' impossible command to "Be perfect ... as your heavenly Father is perfect" (Matt. 5:48). But I've come to regard "consider it pure joy" as far more than a goal. As Judy, Linda, and Donovan demonstrate, believers *really can* experience joy in the toughest situations when they fully surrender themselves to God. In the minds of these three believers, James 1:2 doesn't offer an ideal but simply describes what life was like as they walked with Jesus Christ during the worst of days.

I don't know what I would do if I was in the same situation as these three. In heaven, when I look back and see how my trials shaped and molded me, I am certain I will consider all my trials as joy. But in the here and now, would I do the same? After all, there are many believers I know who have faced similar situations and never rejoiced—either during or after their ordeal. I've seen them turn inward rather than upward. Some ignore God in frustration and risk a jaded, hardened heart. Others try to escape from the pain altogether. Still others crave joy, but hold out for satisfactory answers from God to their "why?" questions.

Judy, Linda, and Donovan offer a joyful alternative. These three "lumps of sunshine" illustrate just how possible it is for ordinary believers, regardless of personality or disposition, to choose to rejoice no matter what they go through and to be genuinely thankful for all they have endured.

Judy was able to experience a deeper joy because of her cancer treatment than she would have been able to without it.

What's more, it was the first time, she realizes, that she fully opened her heart to God and began to see herself as the "apple of God's eye."

Even with a heart that remains delicate and tender, Linda can look back on the past three years and say that she feels blessed. She knows if Bob were still here today that she would not be the same woman in Christ as she has become. On a daily basis, God's joy is proving its mettle—mending, healing, and transforming Linda's broken heart.

Donovan continues to live on in long-term care. Nagging sores recently prevented him from being able to sit up in a wheelchair, forcing him to be confined to his bed for several months. But in spite of these sorts of setbacks, he continues to find joy in the way his life has played out. In spite of losing so much of who he was, he is confident that the joy planted inside of him is preparing him for a glorious future with Christ.

Judy, Linda, and Donovan aren't gluttons for pain—they hope that they never have to face another ordeal as traumatic as the one that they have already gone through. Yet, amazingly, none of them would wish things any different. To them, their trials have reinforced the belief that there is something worth living for, something worth struggling for, and something worth suffering for.

Pummeled by the Sea

During a recent vacation to Cape Cod, Judy was walking alone along the beach on an overcast summer day. On top of the sand, there were tens of thousands of pebbles that had washed up on the shore from the tides. Most were ordinary rocks—

coarse, colorless stones with sharp edges. However, every so often, she would spot a beautiful, shapely pebble. One by one, Judy began collecting these pebbles to take home with her.

Pebbles get smooth and polished by the sea waters when they get caught up in the currents and wear against each other and the sand below. Over time, the endless action of the ocean smoothes their sharp edges and polishes them. The tide sweeps pebbles onto the shore; later, when the tide comes in again, it takes some of these pebbles back out to sea, starting the whole process all over again.

As Judy continued her walk down the beach, she reflected on the symbolism. No one brings home the ugly, coarse stone. The pebbles she was handpicking were the ones that had the toughest times, pummeled over and over again by the sea, sand, and other rocks. But because of the refining process that they went through, they were transformed into pebbles worth keeping.

Judy began to see parallels with the trials that she has endured. Hardship and turmoil are not mere chaos or random events. Instead, they serve a divine purpose — to mold us into the "little Christs" that we were designed to be. It is on believers who surrender themselves and persevere — people like Judy, Linda, and Donovan — that God pours out his joy.

CHAPTER 12

LIVE JOY

That is the joy of the life of God; it is uncrushable life,
and there is never life without joy.
—Oswald Chambers

To pursue joy is to lose it.
The only way to get it is to follow steadily the path of duty,
without thinking of joy.
—Alexander MacLaren

Almost every week, I am reminded of the struggle believers face to live with joy as Judy, Linda, and Donovan have done. Just yesterday, I learned that dear friends of my family, a couple married for nearly fifty years, are getting divorced. From the outside, I can't make any sense of it. They have been active church members for years, the most hospitable and cheerful of hosts, and had a genuine heart for overseas missions. Yet instead of sharing their golden years together, they're now going their separate ways. This most unexpected news illustrates the constant battle that rages for our hearts, even if we wear plastic smiles on the outside. If we don't experience the lasting joy of Jesus Christ at the core of our being, we will seek happiness and fulfillment somewhere, sometime, somehow.

Livestrong is the inspirational slogan of the Lance Armstrong Foundation, made famous through the tens of millions of yellow Livestrong wristbands that have been sold since they were introduced a few years back. The appeal of the campaign is that, whether we are sick or in full health, we all have the desire to "live strong." For those fighting disease, it provides a motivation to press on, regardless of the odds. For the healthy, living strong seems like the way to take matters into our own hands and get out of the thirst, seek, and settle rut we feel trapped in. The message of Livestrong is all about sheer will and self-determination. Or, as the foundation's manifesto says, "It's your life. You will have it your way."

Clint, Mitch, and the other joy-filled Christians I have written about in this book have taken a different path. They know that a believer is called to live joy, not live strong. "It's God's life. He will have it his way" is their countercultural manifesto. For it is only when we are weak in ourselves that we are able to be strong in Christ (2 Cor. 12:10). The joy they experience in the best and worst of times is made possible when they are vulnerable and allow Christ to transform their hearts.

"Living strong" is all about making the most of every moment you have on earth. *Carpe diem* goes the popular Latin phrase.* *Seize the day.* In one sense, Christians should embrace the notion of living life to the fullest. The problem lies in attempting to live out *carpe diem* without submitting our lives to Jesus Christ. We end up living for ourselves and for the

---

*The Lance Armstrong Foundation's annual awards are appropriately called the Carpe Diem awards.

moment. But when we do, we eventually find ourselves back where we started—the dead ends of happiness and personal fulfillment. *Carpe diem* is much like a great dessert recipe that is missing half its ingredients—it's the start of something special, but it's incomplete and unsatisfying on its own.

"Living joy" stands in contrast. We live for eternity, not for ourselves or for the here and now. Yet at the same time, we don't spend our lives behind locked doors waiting for heaven. No, we are fully immersed in every moment of every day, seven days a week, three hundred and sixty-five days a year. We are, in the words of G. K. Chesterton, like "deathless people in an endless tale." For the joy-filled believer, *carpe diem* is thus transformed into something far more meaningful and lasting: *carpe aeternum, gaude diem—seize the eternal, delight in the day.*

Carpe Aeternum

Carpe diem is all about living out my dreams and passions. *Carpe aeternum* involves the same intensity, but the focus is different: pursuing God's will by relinquishing my own. The martyred missionary Jim Elliot summed it up, "Wherever you are, be all there. Live to the hilt every situation you believe to be the will of God."

The Beatitudes are one of the most familiar and sometimes perplexing passages of the Gospels. For centuries, scholars have labored to understand the nuances and the significance of these eight verses of Matthew 5. In addition to the other truths we can discover from these words of Christ, one cannot mistake the clear teaching that Jesus gives on joy. He uses the Beatitudes to say, in effect: if you want to experience my joy and blessing in all its fullness, then here's how. Each verse is much like an artist's brushstroke that, when taken together, form a masterful portrait of living joy. Here are Jesus' words from Matthew 5:3 – 10:

> *Blessed are the poor in spirit,*
>   *for theirs is the kingdom of heaven.*
> *Blessed are those who mourn,*
>   *for they will be comforted.*
> *Blessed are the meek,*
>   *for they will inherit the earth.*
> *Blessed are those who hunger and thirst for righteousness,*
>   *for they will be filled.*
> *Blessed are the merciful,*
>   *for they will be shown mercy.*
> *Blessed are the pure in heart,*
>   *for they will see God.*
> *Blessed are the peacemakers,*
>   *for they will be called sons of God.*
> *Blessed are those who are persecuted because*
>   *of righteousness,*
>   *for theirs is the kingdom of heaven.*

The word at the heart of the Beatitudes is *blessed*. It comes from the original Greek word *makarios*, a term packed with meaning. In ancient Greece, the gods or the elite of society were considered *makarios*. In the Greek translation of the Old Testament, *makarios* referred to righteous Jews who received God's blessings through material wealth. To the average Jew listening to Christ, *makarios* was associated with persons of privilege and prestige, well above their status or peer group.

Consequently, Jesus' words would have been both shocking and liberating to the crowd. God's blessing, he says, has nothing to do with material wealth or earthly rewards; it has everything to do with our hearts.

Some English translations of the Beatitudes translate *makarios* as the word "happy." But given the superficial nature of happiness, this just doesn't work. Happy are those who mourn? Happy are those who are persecuted? Such claims are either naïve or illogical. We end up dumbing down the significance of these words of Jesus in the process. Instead, *makarios* refers to the divine joy that results from living out Christ's teaching. William Barclay observes:

> The Beatitudes in effect say, "O the bliss of being a Christian! O the joy of following Christ!" ... The very form of the Beatitudes is the statement of the joyous thrill and the radiant gladness of the Christian life. In the face of the Beatitudes a gloom-encompassed Christianity is unthinkable.
>
> *Makarios* then describes that joy which has its secret within itself, that joy which is serene and untouchable and self-contained, that joy which is completely independent of all the chances and changes of life ... The Beatitudes are triumphant shouts of bliss for a permanent joy that nothing in the world can ever take away.

Every line of the Beatitudes demonstrates the inseparable bond between experiencing joy and surrender. "Blessed are the poor in spirit," Jesus begins. There is perhaps no better description of a joy-filled Christian than "poor in spirit." After all, in order to allow joy to flow through my heart, I have to be poor, emptying myself out completely so I can be filled by the Holy Spirit. Only when I reach that point of spiritual bankruptcy am I ready to receive the kingdom of heaven.

Each of the verses that follow fills in more and more of what it means to seize the eternal as I surrender my life to Jesus. When I mourn, I have a godly sorrow over sin and the grief that this broken world produces. When I am meek, I walk in humility before God. When I thirst for righteousness, I die to my own desires. When I am merciful, I am self-emptying in showing grace and mercy. When I am pure in heart, I receive God's grace through the blood of Jesus Christ. When I am a peacemaker, my concern is for others around me rather than my own selfish claims.

The promises or rewards that Christ offers in the Beatitudes as we walk in obedience have a mixture of today and the eternal. In the first and last verses, the poor in spirit and the persecuted are offered the kingdom of heaven in the present tense: "Theirs *is* the kingdom of heaven" (italics added). In the middle verses, the promises are all future tense (*"will be"*). The promises in the Beatitudes thus mirror the dual nature of joy—something we can partake and experience partially now, but which is fulfilled in our future in heaven.

Gaude Diem

Playing football with my boys. Getting a new iPod for my birthday. Going out for a night on the town with my wife. Having friends over for dinner. Since I've said all along that happiness is a cheap substitute to lasting joy, one might conclude we are better off by avoiding or ignoring these moments of earthly happiness.

God promises joy as I surrender my life to him. But as I live each day, I see that he graces me with moments of sheer happiness, pleasure, and fun as well. These happy experiences are meant to be viewed as blessings from God, not as noise of the devil. In fact, joy-filled Christians are actually better equipped than anyone else to enjoy the present more—because of our genuine hope and security in the future.* With a certainty in Jesus Christ, I don't need to sweat over the tough issues of life. As a result, I am free to enjoy happy moments without the compulsion to make them my life's ambition. Therefore, the problem with happiness becomes one of attitude and priority, not of avoidance.

I recently watched the 2002 film adaptation of Charles Dickens's *Nicholas Nickleby.* The film chronicles the hard life of Nicholas Nickleby, a young boy cruelly separated from his family who struggles to overcome one hardship after another. At the film's conclusion, when Nicholas is able to rise over adversity and discover happiness, a friend of his named Mr. Crummles tells him, "Happiness is a gift and the trick is not to expect it, but to delight in it when it comes." Mr. Crummles expresses exactly the gracious manner in which we are called to look upon happiness—as a gift to delight in, but not depend on.

*A Barna Research study found that Christians are happier than nonbelievers. In the survey, evangelicals interviewed were almost universally "happy" (99%) and were by far the portion of the population that was most satisfied with their present life (91%). People of non-Christian faiths were slightly less likely than Christians to be happy, while atheists and agnostics were least likely to say that they were happy. (Source: http://www.barna.org/FlexPage.aspx?Page=BarnaUpdate&BarnaUpdateID=119)

Grace transforms the beginning of our life with Christ, cleansing us and equipping us for eternity. I am beginning to understand that joy can transform the redeemed life as well. When we live joy, everything we experience in the present moment has a footing in eternity. The bad and the good. The trials and the triumphs. The sad and the glad. Therefore, trials are not the only experiences engineered and used by God, but happy ones are too. In a most unexpected surprise, happiness is transformed from passing instances of fun into something far more significant. "These moments [of happiness] are filled with eternity," said Chesterton. "These moments are joyful because they do not seem momentary."

Share the Joy

Live strong or live joy? When you and I choose to live joy, then we'll inevitably share our joy. In Matthew 5, Jesus instructs us how to live joy in the Beatitudes; then just four verses later, he tells us what will happen if we live out his commands:

> You are the light of the world. A city on a hill cannot be hidden. Neither do people light a lamp and put it under a bowl. Instead they put it on its stand, and it gives light to everyone in the house. In the same way, let your light shine before others, that they may see your good deeds and praise your Father in heaven. (Matt. 5:14–16)

Evangelicals have always had a special burden and a passion for expressing their faith and being the light of the world. We eagerly share our faith with friends and neighbors, have altar calls on Sunday mornings, and pass out tracts at street corners. Some of us even like to wear our faith on our sleeves, or at least put it on our cars.

I am just old enough to remember the "I Found It" bumper stickers in the 1970s. In the 1980s, *ichthus* fish emblems became a more subtle witness that remains popular today. In the 1990s, the WWJD wristbands and T-shirts proved wildly popular for teens as a way to express their faith. Yet, however effective or ineffective these kinds of expressions may be, I sometimes wonder whether we are missing the point. Shouldn't my greatest distinguisher be the joy I live rather than the fish emblem on my car? After all, when I live the way Christ calls me to, I am going to radiate joy throughout my life. C. H. Spurgeon put it like this:

> Oh, no, there is a charm about holy joy!… Let us sing unto the Lord as long as we live; and, mayhap, some weary sinner, who has discovered the emptiness of sinful pleasure, will say to himself, "Why, after all, there must be something real about the [joy] of these Christians; let me go and learn how I may have it."

When we live joy, then we are transformed into lumps of sunshine, radiating Christ's grace and joy to everyone we come in contact with. Our joy will overflow in worship, in our relationships, in our purpose-driven service to the world around us, and in our creative works.

I suspect that there are few people in the world who have witnessed the transformative power of sharing joy as much as Bruce Marchiano has. Since portraying Jesus in *The Visual Bible: The Gospel according to Matthew* a decade ago, he has spoken to thousands of people worldwide about Christ through his speaking ministry. Whether he is talking to a church in South Africa or at a youth conference in South Carolina, Bruce constantly sees people's lives turned around when they realize the joy that is at the heart of who Jesus Christ is. With excitement in his voice, Bruce exclaims, "I can't tell you how many times I've received a letter with this line in it: 'I've been a Christian for x years, but I never knew who Jesus truly was until now.'"

In fact, Bruce's portrayal of Jesus as a "man of joy" in *The Gospel according to Matthew* was instrumental in transforming an entire church denomination that had been plagued for decades with legalism, ritual, and tradition. As the *Matthew* video spread virally through the denomination's churches, Christ's grace and joy slowly began to overthrow the strongholds of legalism. "I saw this turnaround take place firsthand as I toured through these churches," says Bruce. "I gave the first salvation calls in many of them, preaching a most simple gospel message—the love and joy of Jesus Christ. Literally *en masse*, the people were liberated, the leaders were liberated ... freed from religion, freed unto Jesus."

A Brittle Spirit

Live strong or live joy? Amélie is the main character of the quirky French film *The Fabulous Destiny of Amélie Poulain*. Amélie is a twenty-one-year-old woman living a lonely existence, preferring to be life's spectator rather than be involved with others. Her shut-in neighbor and friend is called the Glass Man, so nicknamed because of a degenerative bone disease that makes his bones prone to breaking. Throughout the film, the Glass Man becomes a keen observer of Amélie's behavior and works to free her from her self-imposed captivity. During the film's climax, he finally speaks what's been on his mind all along, saying, "My little Amélie, you don't have bones of glass ... [But if] you let this chance pass, eventually, your heart will become as dry and brittle as my skeleton."

As I look back upon my journey to joy over the past decade, I am awakened to the fact that we are all posed with the same challenge: claim God's promised gift of joy or else, over the course of a lifetime, let our spirit become dry and brittle. In the end, the choice is ours.

DISCUSSION GUIDE

Chapter 1: A Semi-Charmed Life

1. What is the "thirst, seek, and settle" cycle? Have you experienced this cycle in your life? If so, describe. If not, how have you avoided "settling"?

2. Google the lyrics for "Semi-Charmed Life" by Third Eye Blind. How do these lyrics express the dead ends of a life apart from Christ? Why don't the activities that Third Eye Blind discusses in the song satisfy anyone?

3. Read John 15:11; Luke 6:23; Galatians 5:22–23; Philippians 4:4; and 1 Thessalonians 5:16. Does the joy that is described in these passages reflect what you regularly experience in your Christian walk? If not, do you consider the joy described in these verses as something realistically attainable on a day-in, day-out basis?

4. Wagner says that we often use the word "joy" differently than how it is used in the Bible. Do you think of joy as being the same thing as happiness?

5. How is Solomon an example of a believer living a joyless life? Can you think of other people in the Bible who suffered a similar problem?

6. What are some factors in our world that make it easy for us to become confused with what true joy is?

7. What is "pidgin joy"? What are some ways in which we water down biblical joy?

8. How is joy the "most tangible and transformative gift" that God gives to believers while on earth?

Chapter 2: Nothing but a Yuppie Word

1. What makes you happy? Name at least three things.

2. Is happiness a major motivator of people today? Is it a motivator of you personally? Why or why not?

3. As you reflect on your life over the past week, how much have you focused your time and energies on "being happy"?

4. Think of recent television ads you've seen. How do these ads emphasize happiness as a motivation for people buying their products? Give some examples.

5. What are different ways in which people pursue happiness?

6. "I deserve it" is a common expression we hear in contemporary culture. When do we feel that we "deserve" something? From Christ's perspective, do we ever "deserve" anything?

7. Culture tells us to "find something that makes you happy and do it." Is this biblical? Back up your answer with Scripture.

8. The U.S. Constitution implies that the "pursuit of happiness" is a right given to us by God. Do you agree or

disagree? Can you offer any Bible verses to support your answer?

9. According to Wagner, what are the two basic rules that most people follow to pursue happiness? As you look on your life, do you see yourself following these rules, consciously or subconsciously?

10. Read Job 20:5. Does happiness last? Explain your answer.

11. Describe a circumstance in your life in which you experienced happiness, only to see it vanish as time passed. Was this avoidable?

Chapter 3: Flickers of a Far-Off Country

1. Read Psalms 65:8, 13; 66:1; 96:12; 98:4; and 100:1. How is joy experienced through God's creation? Have you experienced joy in a manner as Wagner did in the Rocky Mountains?

2. What is "common joy"? How does this differ from the joy experienced inside the heart of a believer?

3. Read Psalms 4:7; 5:11; 16:11; 19:18; 21:6; and 28:7. How do these verses back up the idea that when the eternal touches our world, then joy is the inevitable result?

4. Describe the scene in *The Shawshank Redemption* discussed in the book. Why did Andy believe it was worth it to play the music over the loudspeakers, even knowing his certain punishment?

5. This chapter talks about the impact of the music of Henryk Górecki in the 1990s. Has music ever touched you in a similar way?

6. John Calvin wrote, "There is not one blade of grass, there is no color in this world that is not intended to make us rejoice." How does Philippians 4:4 help back up Calvin's perspective?

7. What is the major purpose of common joy?

8. Does common joy satisfy? Why or why not? Give an example from your life.

9. What is a danger of focusing too much on common joy?

10. *Optional activity*: Watch the opera singing clip from *The Shawshank Redemption*. (Note: This film is extremely well made and has a powerful story line related to common joy and hope. However, note that the film has an R rating for graphic prison violence and strong profanity.)

11. *Optional activity*: Listen to Henryk Górecki's Symphony 3, *Sorrowful Songs*.

Chapter 4: A Blessed Invasion

1. Read John 15:11; 16:24; 17:13; and Romans 15:13. Is joy a constant presence in the life of a believer?

2. Based on this chapter, how would you define joy? Has your understanding of joy changed since you started reading this book?

3. What are six key qualities of biblical joy?

4. If joy is a permanent presence in the life of a believer, why do we find it so difficult to experience continual joy?

5. Describe the similarities between grace and joy as manifestations of God's love.

6. If you had to share with another Christian three key facts of joy, what would they be?

7. Read Nehemiah 8:10. How can joy be our strength?

8. Compare and contrast biblical joy and happiness. How are they alike? Different?

Chapter 5: Christ Overjoyed

1. Read Hebrews 1:9. Why is this verse a key in understanding Jesus during his earthly ministry?

2. Before reading this chapter, did you think of Jesus as a "man of joy"? Why or why not?

3. Read Luke 1:46 – 49; 2:10, 13 – 14, 19 – 20, 25 – 26. Who experienced joy? Why? What insight do these verses give us concerning the nature of the incarnate Christ?

4. Read Isaiah's prophetic description of the Messiah in Isaiah 53. How does this characterization (particularly verse 2) compare to your understanding of who Jesus Christ was during his earthly ministry?

5. What drew people to Jesus Christ during his three-year ministry on earth? What does Wagner believe was the most significant attractor?

6. Read Hebrews 12:2. Was Jesus able to experience joy in the Garden of Gethsemane, trial, and crucifixion? Why or why not?

7. Can you think of difficult experiences you endured because of the joy you knew you would experience later?

8. Read Luke 15:6, 9, 23 – 24 (or read all of Luke 15). In these verses, Jesus talks about the joy in heaven when sinners repent and come to him. What joy did you feel when you or a person close to you became a believer? Explain.

9. *Optional activity*: Watch the Visual Bible's *The Gospel according to Mathew*, focusing on how Jesus is portrayed as a "man of joy."

Chapter 6: Lumps of Sunshine

1. What qualities of Clint appeal to Wagner so much?

2. What nickname did C. H. Spurgeon call a joyful man he knew? Why is this moniker such a descriptive term for a joy-filled person?

3. What is the "Pleasantville Effect"? Can you identify two Christians who have this effect on people with whom they come into contact? Explain.

4. Do you think others around you see you as a "lump of sunshine"? If not, what is getting in the way of joy?

5. Describe the bishop in *Les Misérables*. What evidence was there that he was a joy-filled person?

6. How does outwardly expressed joy differ from charm or charisma?

7. Why is joy such an important characteristic for Christians to exhibit in their lives?

8. *Optional activities*: Watch beginning scenes of the 1998 film adaptation of *Les Misérables*. Or read the opening chapters of the unabridged version of Victor Hugo's *Les Misérables* that center on the life of the bishop. Share your thoughts.

Chapter 7: The "S" Word

1. Are there times in your life in which you have experienced joy and peace in the midst of stressful circumstances? What were the key reasons for this attitude?

2. Jesus says "follow me" over twenty times in the Gospels. Who obeyed and simply followed Christ? Who chose not to listen to Christ's words because they believed the cost to be too great? What was the long-term effect of their decision?

3. Read Luke 9:23 – 25. Practically speaking, how are we to respond to this call in today's world?

4. What is surrender?

5. Can a burnt offering, a living sacrifice, and carrying a cross be expressions of joy? How?

6. What crisis of belief does Phil Connors face in *Groundhog Day*? How did he ultimately find fulfillment? How does the fictional account of Connors help illustrate the need to be surrendered to Christ?

7. What is the relationship between joy and surrender? Explain.

8. Read John 15:1 – 11. How can our joy be complete?

9. What is a "tweener"? Are you a "tweener" today? If not, have there been periods of your life where you would describe yourself as a "tweener"?

10. Can you name things in your life that you do not want to give up that may be keeping you from fully surrendering your life to Christ? If so, what impact do these things have on the joy you are or are not experiencing?

11. Have you ever fully given yourself to Christ, and are you committed to living as a disciple?

12. *Optional activity*: Watch *Groundhog Day*.

Chapter 8: Driven by Purpose

1. Do you feel as if you are living out your life's purpose? Explain.

2. What is the relationship between joy and purpose? What examples can you think of in your life or in Scripture that back up that interrelationship?

3. Why isn't a purpose enough to guarantee a joy-filled life?

4. What does the book of Ecclesiastes say about the purpose of life? According to Solomon, what activities lead to dead ends? And, in the end, what fulfills?

5. What does the experience of Eric Liddell teach us about discovering joy when we live out God's purpose?

6. How does living out our God-given purpose enable us to experience a special joy? Name five factors.

7. Think of someone you know (or a person from the Bible) who is living out God's purpose for them. Do they exhibit joy?

8. Read Isaiah 40:28–31. How does this passage teach us how to get beyond an "underpurposed" life?

9. According to Martin Luther, how can we find joy in serving God? Are some vocations more joyful than others?

10. In the chapter, how did Mitch find joy even though he could not live out his purpose to the extent that he longed for?

11. *Optional activity*: Watch *Chariots of Fire.*

Chapter 9: Joy Busters

1. Identify the five "joy busters" that Wagner discusses in the chapter. How would you rank their influence on your life? Explain.

2. Fear, uncertainty, and doubt (FUD) can rob us of our joy. What examples in the Scriptures are there of God's people being paralyzed with fear? Have you had similar experiences? How did you deal with them?

3. Thomas was plagued with fear and doubt in events chronicled in John 14 and 20. What can we learn from these two experiences?

4. How much of a problem does your church have with a "gloom and doom" mentality? Would a visitor coming to your church on Sunday sense joy or grumbling?

5. Why is forgiveness of yourself and others so critical to experiencing God's joy?

6. What are the two options we have when we experience a "joy buster"?

7. What does Wagner say is the ultimate source of things that rob us of joy? How does C. S. Lewis's classic book *The Great Divorce* illustrate this truth?

8. What steps did Wagner take to deal with his struggles concerning joy, even when he didn't have all of the answers?

9. *Optional activity*: Read C. S. Lewis, *The Great Divorce*.

Chapter 10: Glory Days

1. In 29 of the 39 books of the Old Testament, the children
   of Israel are reminded "to remember" the glory days of
   God's faithfulness. The Israelites are to remember how
   the Lord cared for them in the past so they can have faith
   and hope to live in their present situation. What are some
   glory days in your past? Do they help you to live a more
   faithful life now?

2. Tom and Red in *Seabiscuit* illustrate how persons can
   struggle with living a meaningful life after having a great
   deal of success. How can a believer's faith in Christ help
   the person avoid a similar fate?

3. How would you compare the way Veronica Lake
   dealt with a declining career with the way Clint did in
   chapter 6?

4. How does looking back to the glory days cause us to miss
   opportunities that are available now?

5. Read Luke 17:32 – 33. How does Lot's wife warn us of
   the dangers of living in the past?

6. How does past-tense living rob us of our joy? How does
   past-tense living make surrender impossible?

7. Read Philippians 3:12 – 16. What can we glean from
   Paul's testimony to apply to our lives?

8. *Optional activity*: Listen to Bruce Springsteen's "Glory
   Days" song.

Chapter 11: Proving Grounds

1. Read James 1:2 and 1 Peter 1:6. Are James and Peter being realistic? Do you find these passages encouraging when you face trials? Why or why not?

2. "Don't Worry, Be Happy" was a popular song from the 1990s. Is James 1:2 merely a Christianized version of the same sentiment? Why or why not?

3. Recount the stories of Judy, Linda, and Donovan. How did they respond to the trials they experienced? How is their response more than just putting on a plastic smile?

4. How can Judy's words, "It is not about me. It is all about him," help us in difficult situations? How did these words help Judy have lasting joy?

5. What is "Indy joy" as described in this chapter? What is the difference between Indy joy and real joy?

6. Have you or Christians you have known become embittered through hardship?

7. Can grief and joy coexist? Explain and give an example from Scripture or your own life. Read, for example, Habakkuk 3:17 – 19.

8. Who does the author say are the persons who experience God's joy? Would you count yourself as one of those persons? If not, how can you become one who constantly experiences God's joy?

Chapter 12: Live Joy

1. What is the underlying worldview of "living strong"? Is this way of life compatible with Christianity?

2. What does *carpe aeternum, gaude diem* mean? How does it differ from *carpe diem*?

3. Read Matthew 5:3 – 10. What does the word "blessed" mean? Why is it problematic to translate it as "happy"?

4. How do the Beatitudes help us to understand what it means to *carpe aeternum, gaude diem*?

5. How do the Beatitudes convey the interwoven relationship between joy and surrender?

6. How are believers to approach happy experiences? Should they avoid or embrace them?

7. Why are joy-filled Christians better equipped to enjoy the present than others?

8. What one or two principles will you take away from this book to enable you to live out joy consistently in your Christian walk?

BIBLICAL REFERENCES ON JOY

Joy is a running theme throughout all of the Scriptures. Below are some of the major references, categorized by topic.

Joy is the nature of God in believers (ch. 4): Neh. 8:10; Ps. 4:7; John 3:29; 15:11; Gal. 5:22; 1 Thess. 1:6.

Joy is received through surrender and obedience (ch. 7): Ps. 19:8; 30:11; 97:11; 118:15; 132:16; Prov. 10:28; Matt. 5:3 – 10; 13:44; John 17:13.

Joy can be found in the midst of trials (ch. 11): Job 3:7; 6:10; Luke 6:23; John 16:20; 2 Cor. 7:4; 8:2; 1 Thess. 5:16; Heb. 12:2; James 1:2; 1 Peter 1:6.

Joy is shared with other believers (ch. 4): Luke 1:58; Rom. 15:32; 16:19; 2 Cor. 1:24; 2:3; 7:4 – 7; Phil. 1:4, 26; 2:2, 29; 4:1; 1 Thess. 2:19 – 20; 3:9; 2 Tim. 1:4; Philem. 7; 1 John 1:4; 2 John 12; 3 John 3 – 4.

Joy is found in the presence of God (ch. 4): Lev. 9:24; 1 Chron. 16:27; 29:22; Ps. 16:11; 21:6; 94:19; Acts 2:28; Jude 24.

Joy is found through worship (ch. 4): 1 Chron. 16:33; Job 8:21; 33:26; Ps. 27:6 – 7; 33:3; 43:4; 47:5; 67:4; 71:23; 81:1; 86:4; 89:12; 92:4; 95:1; 98:6; Isa. 12:6; Luke 24:52.

We can look forward to a joyful future (ch. 4): Isa. 26:19; 35:10; 51:11; 60:5; 61:7; John 16:22.

"Common joy" is found for all people (ch. 3): Ps. 96:12; 98:8; Acts 14:17.

Joy is a key quality of the kingdom of God (ch. 12): Matt. 5:3 – 10; Rom. 14:17.

Losing joy (chs. 9, 10): Job 9:25; Gal. 4:15.

Fleeting nature of happiness (ch. 2): Job 20:5.

Joy as part of the nature of Jesus the Son and God the Father (chs. 4, 5): Zeph. 3:17; Heb. 1:9; Ps. 45:7; Heb. 12:2.

Joy is a result of God's blessing (ch. 4): 1 Chron. 12:40; 2 Chron. 30:26; Ezra 6:16; Neh. 8:12 – 17; 12:43; Esth. 9:17; Ps. 21:1; 126:3.

Joy found in God's Word (chs. 4, 9): Ps. 71:23; 31:7; 33:1 – 4; 119:111, 162; Jer. 15:16; 1 Peter 1:8.

ENDNOTES

Chapter 1: A Semi-Charmed Life

Page 14: C. S. Lewis, *The Screwtape Letters* (San Francisco: HarperSanFrancisco, 2001), 60.

Page 14: Third Eye Blind, "Semi-Charmed Life," *Third Eye Blind* (Elektra, 1997).

Page 14: Tony Campolo, *Seven Deadly Sins* (Colorado Springs: Victor, 1987).

Page 16: *The Princess Bride*, directed by Rob Reiner, 1987.

Page 18: *Rolling Stone*, 1991. Quoted on *switchfoot.com/musicframe.htm*.

Page 20: G. K. Chesterton, *Orthodoxy* (Garden City, N.Y.: Doubleday [Image Books], 1959), 160. Quoted in Sherwood Eliot Wirt, *Jesus: Man of Joy* (Nashville: Nelson, 1991), 73.

Chapter 2: Nothing but a Yuppie Word

Page 24: *Buffy the Vampire Slayer*, "Becoming: Part 2" (#2.22), 1997.

Page 25: Frank Furedi, "Why the 'Politics of Happiness' Makes Me Mad," *London Daily Telegraph* (see *www.spiked-online.com/index.php?/site /article/311*).

Page 27: *24*, episode "2X10" (original airdate: Jan. 14, 2003).

Page 34: Sophia Hawthorne, ed., *Passages from the American Note-Books of Nathaniel Hawthorne* (Boston: Houghton, Mifflin & Co, 1883). Available online at *www.eldritchpress.org/nh/pfanb01.html#g5126*.

Chapter 3: Flickers of a Far-Off Country

Page 38: Quote can be found at *ctlibrary.com/3763*.

Page 38: Gerald Kennedy, *The Lion and the Lamb* (Nashville: Abingdon-Cokesbury, 1950), 85. Quoted in Wirt, *Jesus: Man of Joy*, 73.

Page 39: C. S. Lewis, *Narrative Poems*, "Dymer" (New York: Harcourt Brace Jovanovich, 1964, 1st pub. 1926), verse 10.

Page 39: C. S. Lewis, *The Pilgrim's Regress* (Grand Rapids: Eerdmans, 1960).

Page 39: Adrian Thomas, "Intense Joy and Profound Rhythm: An Introduction to the Music of Henryk Mikolaj Górecki," *Polish Music Journal* 6, no. 2 (Winter 2003).

Page 41: *The Shawshank Redemption*, directed by Frank Darabont, 1994.

Page 42: David Kopplin, "The Concept of Time in the Music of Henryk Górecki," *Polish Music Journal* 6, no. 2 (Winter 2003). See *www.usc.edu/dept/polish_music/PMJ/issue/6.2.03/Kopplin.html*.

Page 42: Chuck Colson, *How Now Shall We Live?* (Wheaton, Ill.: Tyndale, 1999), 438.

Page 43: C. S. Lewis, *The Weight of Glory and Other Addresses* (Grand Rapids: Eerdmans, 1949), 5.

Page 44: C. S. Lewis, *Letters to Malcolm: Chiefly on Prayer* (San Diego: Harvest, Harcourt Brace Jonanovich, 1964), 93.

Chapter 4: A Blessed Invasion

Page 48: Oswald Chambers, *The Best from All His Books, Volume I*, ed. Harry Verploegh (Nashville: Nelson, 1987), 188.

Page 49: Charles Spurgeon, "Christ's Joy and Ours," The Spurgeon Archive: *www.spurgeon.org*.

Page 49: I want to credit Oswald Chambers for his general ideas on this concept of joy. Based on ideas from *The Complete Works of Oswald Chambers, The Psychology of Redemption* (Grand Rapids: Discovery House, 2000), 1102.

Page 49: Oswald Chambers, *The Best from All His Books, Volume I*, 188.

Page 53: Philip Yancey, *What's So Amazing About Grace?* (Grand Rapids: Zondervan, 1997), 26.

Page 54: Charles Spurgeon, "Christ's Joy and Ours," The Spurgeon Archive: *www.spurgeon.org.*

Page 55: Oswald Chambers, *The Best from All His Books, Volume I,* 190.

Page 57: Charles Spurgeon, "Joy, a Duty," The Spurgeon Archive: *www. spurgeon.org/sermons/2405.htm.*

Page 59: C. S. Lewis, *Surprised by Joy* (San Diego: Harcourt Brace, 1984), 18.

Chapter 5: Christ Overjoyed

Page 67: Bruce Marchiano, *In the Footsteps of Jesus* (Eugene, Ore.: Harvest House, 2001), 77.

Page 68: Ibid., 82.

Chapter 6: Lumps of Sunshine

Page 71: Charles Spurgeon, "Joy, a Duty."

Page 72: Ibid.

Page 72: Ibid.

Page 76: Victor Hugo, *Les Misérables,* trans. Charles E. Wilbour (New York: Barnes & Noble, 1996), 90.

Page 78: Oswald Chambers, *The Best from All His Books, Volume II,* ed. Harry Verploegh (Nashville: Nelson, 1989), 163.

Page 79: Victor Hugo, *Les Misérables,* 47.

Chapter 7: The "S" Word

Page 92: C. S. Lewis, *Mere Christianity* (Nashville: Broadman & Holman, 1996), 60.

Page 93: Paraphrased from Lewis, *The Screwtape Letters.*

Page 94: Oswald Chambers, *The Best from All His Books, Volume I,* 346.

Page 95: Dietrich Bonhoeffer, *The Cost of Discipleship* (New York: Collier, 1963), 90.

Chapter 8: Driven by Purpose

Page 99: *Chariots of Fire*, directed by Hugh Hudson, 1981.

Page 101: Ibid.

Page 102: Oswald Chambers, *The Best from All His Books, Volume II*, 163.

Page 104: Martin Luther, ed. Ewald M. Plass "Faith Sanctifies All Work ...," Sect. 1699, *What Luther Says: An Anthology Vol. 2* (St. Louis: Concordia, 1959), 560. Quoted in Tom Browning, "The History of the Reformation: How Christ Restored the Gospel to His Church," Threshhold: *www.monergism.com/thethreshold/articles/onsite/browning/Lesson10.pdf.*

Page 105: Ibid.

Page 105: See *The Encyclopedia of Christian Quotations*, Mark Water comp. (Grand Rapids: Baker, 2000), 537.

Chapter 9: Joy Busters

Page 121: The quote can be found at *www.brainyquote.com/quotes/authors/h/h_l_mencken.html.*

Page 124: C. S. Lewis, *The Great Divorce* (New York: Macmillan, 1946), 62.

Page 125: Lewis, *The Screwtape Letters*, 40.

Chapter 10: Glory Days

Page 133: C. S. Lewis, *Letters to an American Lady* (Grand Rapids: Eerdmans, 1978), 99.

Page 134: C. S. Lewis, *Prince Caspian* (New York: Macmillan, 2000), 143.

Page 137: Bonhoeffer, *The Cost of Discipleship*, 62 – 63.

Page 138: From an unpublished poem by Owen Barfield. Quoted in C. S. Lewis, *Present Concerns: Essays by C. S. Lewis*, (London: Fount Paperbacks, 1986), 59.

Chapter 11: Proving Grounds

Page 142: A Swahili phrase made popular from Disney's *The Lion King.*

Page 150: C. S. Lewis, *The Problem of Pain* (New York: Macmillan, 1962), 120.

Chapter 12: Live Joy

Page 159: Elizabeth Elliot, *Through the Gates of Splendor* (Wheaton, Ill.: Tyndale, 1981), 20.

Page 161: William Barclay, "The Gospel of Matthew," *The Daily Study Bible*, Vol. 1 (Edinburgh: Saint Andrew, 1962), 83–85. Quoted in Wirt, *Jesus: Man of Joy*, 67–68.

Page 163: *Nicholas Nickleby*, directed by Douglas McGrath, 2002.

Page 164: Chesterton, *Heretics*, ch. 7 (Project Gutenberg: *www.gutenberg .org/etext/470*).

Page 165: C. H. Spurgeon, "Joy, a Duty," The Spurgeon Archive: *www.spurgeon.org/sermons/2405.htm.*

Page 167: *Le fabuleux destin d'Amélie Poulain*, directed by Jean-Pierre Jeunet, 2001.

COMING
JULY 2008

SAMPLE CHAPTER OF

THE
EXPEDITIONARY
MAN

HARDWIRED FOR ADVENTURE

I believe it is in our nature to explore, to reach out into the unknown.
The only true failure would be to not explore at all.
—**Ernest Shackleton**

You are my greatest adventure, and I almost missed it.
—**Mr. Incredible to his family in *The Incredibles***

A man is hardwired for adventure. I see evidence of this truth everywhere. It is found in the films men love to watch and the sports they pursue. I spot it in the gleam of my friend's eye as he talks about his career change. And, more personally, I see it in the exploits that are written on my heart.

The question every Christian man wrestles with, however, is what to do with these desires. Is it possible for a man to pursue a life of adventure when he is married, raising kids, and has a mortgage to pay? How do I prioritize, a man asks himself, what I am driven to do with what I am responsible for?

Some men choose to live out their dreams, no matter the cost. Others stifle them in order to be a good family man.

Many attempt to balance their pursuits with their responsibilities as husband and father. The problem is that when you look at the lives of men in the church today, nothing seems balanced at all. Too many Christian homes are falling apart. Too many youth are abandoning their faith as they hit college campuses. Too many Christian men are leading unfulfilled, mundane lives.

This battle of "adventure vs. duty" is brilliantly depicted in the Pixar film *The Incredibles*. The film chronicles the struggle of Bob Parr, a man who gives up his livelihood as superhero Mr. Incredible and settles down into a normal suburban life. But, after fifteen years, Parr's life has become one of monotony, boredom, and purposelessness. Working as an insurance agent, he spends his days cramped in a tiny cubicle, lost inside a faceless bureaucracy. Parr goes through the motions at work and zones out at home. In his glory days as Mr. Incredible, Bob Parr saved the world by capturing evil criminals. Now, in the words of his wife, his humdrum charge is to "save the world, one policy at a time."

Bob's thirst for adventure, however, can't be stomped out entirely, and it eventually surfaces again. Bob and his buddy Lucius (ex-superhero Frozone) go out every Tuesday night together. Their wives think they go bowling, but the two are actually listening to the police scanner so they can go fight criminals or help out in an emergency. Over time, Bob's "recreational" crime fighting ends up becoming his all-consuming focus when he takes on a new assignment as a superhero behind his wife's back. But, when the mission goes awry, his family is nearly destroyed in the process.

Bob Parr tried to live a normal, quiet life. It was a life that his family and others expected of him. But, just like the real world, a man cannot live forever inside the walls of expectation. Adventure inevitably springs from the soul of a man.

Adventure in All Shapes and Forms

Let's face it: adventure just isn't the same nowadays. For nearly all of human history, this word signified real risk, genuine danger, and life-or-death competition. Uncharted lands were explored. A family's survival depended on defeating enemies. And hard work was essential to surviving in a hostile environment.

While most men wouldn't want to turn back the clock on the comfort and conveniences of the twenty-first century, they do grieve over what has been lost in a tame world. In fact, our situation today is reminiscent of a scene in the Jim Carrey film *The Truman Show*, when a young Truman eagerly tells his teacher that he wants to be another Magellan. Dousing all of his enthusiasm, she responds, "Oh, you're too late! There's nothing left to explore!" Like Truman, a man can feel as if he was born too late, that there's nothing left but a giant "Been There, Done That" sticker slapped on the earth.

God designed men to be resilient and adaptable creatures, however. Even if the grand discoveries of the past are now only found in history books, adventure is still alive and well in the heart of a man. In fact, the experience of the past century has shown that if a man can't find adventure in his daily life, he will manufacture it in his career, recreation, and, for Christians, a ministry.

Career

It's not just a job, it's an adventure. That slogan may be a tired old U.S. Army advertising catchphrase, but it does get to the heart of what a man looks for in life. Every man wants an adventure for a career. Even the way in which we talk about business today reveals this reality. The corporate world is often portrayed in the media as a battleground for modern "warriors." Entrepreneurs are the heroic explorers, charting new waters in technology and the marketplace. Corporate pirates are the evil, greedy villains bent on world domination. Certainly in the Silicon Valley world I used to belong to, the passion for innovation in the early days of the web had all the spirit of the inventers of yesteryear. My coworkers and I truly felt as if we were living through something special, and we were all thrilled to be a part of it.

For a man spending most of his waking hours in this kind of environment, the idea of corporate warfare is intoxicating. The drive for a successful career is often too potent and seductive for him to resist. He is determined to win in the marketplace against his competition. He is motivated by the challenge of completing a major project on time and on budget. If he needs to, a man will work eighty hours a week to build his career and outshine his coworkers. None of these are "adventures" in the classic sense. And, unless a man is a physician, his job is probably not a matter of life and death. But that doesn't really matter to him. Whether a man leads a Fortune 500 company, sells copiers, or crunches numbers for a living, his career can challenge, give purpose, and provide an identity for him.

Recreation

Not all men have jobs that challenge. Some men experience no adventure at all in their profession. Like Bob Parr in *The Incredibles*, they put in their time simply to bring home a paycheck. "I owe, I owe, so off to work I go" reads an old bumper sticker. For this man, adventure is something experienced on the weekends, manufactured through sports, hobbies, and other recreational activities. To make it through life, he gets enough of an "adventure fix" to make it through the drudgery or pressures of the work week. Some of the most popular pastimes include:

- *Outdoor recreation.* Because so much of work today is performed behind a desk, outdoor activities and sports are one of the most coveted outlets for a man. The Field & Stream crowd goes fishing and hunting. The Soldiers of Fortune play paintball in the woods. The Athletes go mountain climbing, skiing, or cycling. Whatever the activity, outdoor physical activity somehow recaptures the age-old spirit of adventure and exploration in a man.

- *Digital entertainment.* Within our technology-driven world, increasing numbers are letting their X-Box game consoles, televisions, and computers do the adventuring for them. While most people think of video games as a domain dominated by teenagers, the statistics reveal a far different reality. Over four out of ten gamers are over the age of thirty-five years, and a whopping 75 percent of all heads of households play regularly.

- *Youth sports.* Coaching in youth sports is another magnet, particularly for ex-athletes desiring the thrill of competition that they once had in their school days. Why else would a grown man become passionate about the success or failure of his Little League team? Deep inside, there's something far more at stake for him than whether a bunch of elementary school kids win or lose a ballgame. To him, it's personal.

- *Spectator sports.* Televised team sports may be the single most popular outlet for men. While the outdoor sportsman may scoff at the idea of real adventure while sitting on a couch in front of the television, the sports fan sees things differently. In his eyes, he is living out the highs and lows of competition, risk, and sense of belonging as he follows his favorite sports team.*

Ministry

While some men may get involved in church ministries out of duty or obligation, others do so because it's a true adventure. A man's passion may be, for example, to lead an evangelism campaign, counsel other men in church, or volunteer time with a prison ministry. Being involved with a growing ministry can be an all-out thrill ride for a man. In our throwaway society, it is his chance to feel a part of something eternally significant.

*It's no coincidence that the invention and popularity of modern spectator sports has coincided with the increasing domestication of life. Men may have more free time to spend on recreation than they did two centuries years ago, but they have an increasing need for it as well.

Pursuits

I have pursued adventure in most every way imaginable in my life. Back in my early twenties, I did what others around me thought was crazy—I organized and rode on two cross-country bicycle trips to raise money for a missions hospital in Haiti.

After I jumped off the bike and got married, I wasn't content to settle in one place for life. There was just too much of the world to see. So, during our twenties, my wife and I moved frequently, living in Washington, D.C., Colorado, the Midwest, and New England.

Eventually, after we had children, I began to quench my thirst for adventure in my career. Driven to succeed in the high-tech world, there was always a challenge that would keep me working long hours: inventing a software product, moving to a fast-rising internet company in Silicon Valley, and then climbing up the corporate ladder. I worked hard to be a good husband and father, and I was involved in various church ministries. But, truth be told, my real passion was in my career.

However, as the years passed, I started to change. As I matured in my walk with Christ, I realized that in my drive to succeed in the workplace, I was neglecting my family at home. My marriage suffered. My boys were growing up quickly, and if I didn't make changes, I would miss out on their childhood. Over time, my passion for workplace success was superseded by the desire to be a good father and husband. But, in the process, I slowly began to lose the spirit of adventure that I had always had. Under the pressures of being a godly husband, raising three boys, and paying the bills, I gave up my aspirations and goals. I set out to do "the responsible thing." My thirst for adventure seemed incompatible with my calling at home; my only choice, I started to believe, was to give it all up.

I changed jobs. I moved from a dream role in a high profile company to a downer of a job at Acme, Inc. On paper, the new position seemed ideal given my family focus: decent salary, no travel, and flexibility in telecommuting for much of the week. But I hated it. My role wasn't challenging or stimulating, and the company was going nowhere. I used to meet with industry movers and shakers; now I was working on a product no one cared about or even heard of. My former office was bright, hip, and located in the heart of Silicon Valley; the new office was in a depressing brownstone that looked like something out of the *Mod Squad.*

My life started to resemble that of Bob Parr in *The Incredibles.* One scene of the film in particular captures the restlessness that stirred in my heart at that point in my life. Arriving home from work, Bob notices a little boy from the neighborhood staring at him as he gets out of his car. You see, the boy once saw Bob lift up the car over his head, and so he regularly rode over on his tricycle to see more. When Bob asks the boy what he is waiting for, he responds, "I don't know. Something amazing, I guess." Bob sighs, "Me too, kid." Like Bob, I was waiting for something spectacular to happen in my life. I believed I was in the job God wanted me to be in at the time, but I was convinced that there had to be more.

Years passed, and the desire for adventure swirled inside of me once again. I was at a point in my career where I should have been most concerned with playing it safe. After all, we had just moved into a new home, and my kids were entering their teen years. But common sense, I am discovering, is more often than not the archenemy of following Jesus Christ. Oswald Chambers explains, "The temptation is to yield to ordinary common sense rather than wait for God to fulfill his purpose. God's order comes to us through the haphazard." Feeling led by God, I exchanged my safe, salaried career in for a long shot at writing books for a living. But, this time around, I was determined to keep my aspirations in line with my family priorities.

Going Solo

It's been three years since that decision point in my life. Looking back today, what is more striking to me than the actual decision I made is how I made it: I was defining adventure purely in solo terms. Adventure, for me, was what I wanted to do with *my* career, *my* ministry, and *my* hobbies. My dreams were personal quests—to be a full-time Christian author, to launch a new discipleship ministry, to ride my bike across the United States again, to climb Mount Aconcagua. Today, as I talk with other men, I realize that I am not alone.

Solo climbing is a type of mountaineering that involves going up a trail or cliff unsupported, not belayed by anyone else. Many consider it the ultimate mountain climbing test. Requiring skill, stamina, and self-reliance, the challenge is entirely personal; it's a man versus a mountain. If you compare a man's outlook on life to a mountain ascent, a man tends to think like a solo climber. This teeth-clenched, single-mindedness— whether it is on a mountain or in an office—is second nature to any man.

Consider, for example, John Eldredge's challenge at the close of *Wild at Heart*: "If you had permission to do what you really want to do, what would you do?... What is written on your heart? What makes you come alive?" Every man I've talked to who has read his book always answers Eldredge's question in solo terms.

Take, for example, my friend Mitch. His passion is to quit his sales job and enter the full-time ministry. Robert wants to launch a new company based on an invention he developed. My buddy Don is driven to start a new twentysomething outreach program at his church. No man I've encountered thinks of his family as being integral to the adventure he is seeking. Adventure is "out there" over the horizon; family is back at home. In fact, when thinking of his family, a man is usually gauging the negative impact that the pursuit of his dreams will have on his wife and children.

George Costanza in *Seinfeld* expresses the compartmentalizing that can take place in a man's life when his adventures are kept separate from his family. In the "Pool Boy" episode, George is stressed when his fiancée wants to hang around with his longtime circle of friends. Up until this point, George has successfully divided his life into Relationship George and Independent George. Now, he's terrified at the prospect of having these two worlds collide. In desperation, he exclaims, "If Relationship George walks through this door, he will kill Independent George. A George divided against itself cannot stand!"

Some men share George's fear and will do anything to prevent the two worlds from colliding. A second group of men give up altogether on the idea of adventure being compatible with family responsibilities. A final group attempts to balance these competing priorities. I call these three responses the Rugged Individualist, the Expectations Guy, and the Balanced Man.

The Rugged Individualist

A man can develop such a passion for pursuing adventure in his life that he becomes consumed by it, leaving his family behind in the process. Maybe he turns into a workaholic. Or perhaps he spends all his free time in a ministry or a hobby. The Rugged Individualist gives lip service to his family and may genuinely desire to be a good husband and father. But, deep down, a family feels like deadweight for a man who wants to pursue solo adventures.

The legendary Ernest Shackleton is the "poster child" of the Rugged Individualist. An Artic explorer, Shackleton is most remembered for his brilliant leadership during the ill-fated *Endurance* expedition to the South Pole in 1914 – 16. During the voyage, the ship that Shackleton and his crew were on became trapped in the ice and eventually sank. For nearly two years, Shackleton kept his team working together over ice, land, and sea, overcoming countless death-defying encounters, and enabling every member of his crew to survive the ordeal. For his mastery of survival and leadership skills, Shackleton is held up by many as one of the greatest heroes of our time. Even James Dobson writes a glowing afterward of the man in *Endurance: Shackleton's Incredible Voyage*.

Yet, in spite of his legendary skills, Shackleton was a lousy husband and father. He loved his family, but he was a restless spirit at home. After his *Endurance* expedition, he attempted a normal life back in England. It didn't take. Shackleton longed for another expedition, and within a few years, left again for Antarctica. "I suppose I'm just good as an explorer and nothing else," confessed Shackleton in a recent biographical film. Shackleton meant well, but his drive for adventure caused him to all but abandon his family in the process. A man doesn't need to travel to the South Pole, however, to neglect his family in pursuit of individual fulfillment. He can just as easily do it while sleeping under the same roof.

The Expectations Guy

Other men, motivated by burden, responsibility, or earnest dedication to their family, feel as if they have no other choice but to suppress their desire for adventure. They focus instead on being simply a good husband and father. This man lives out his life based on other people's expectations, whether it is his wife, his church, or even (what he perceives as) God himself.

A man's decision to put his family first is honorable and a demonstration of his spiritual leadership. However, like Mr. Incredible himself, he needs to be aware of the inherent dangers of living based on the opinions of others. Not only does a man risk wasting his talents and his calling (Matt. 25:14–30), but he also can become a time bomb waiting to explode.

The Balanced Man

Within the church, movements like Promise Keepers and Man in the Mirror have had great success in challenging men to glorify God through their work, giving priority to their family, and serving Christ through a ministry. To many evangelical men today, "balance" has become the mantra, the key to an effective Christian man's life—dividing time and priority between work, family, and a ministry.

The idea of a balanced approach certainly sounds good. The problem, however, is in actually pulling it off. Frankly, I am convinced that balance doesn't *really* work in the real world. Balance deals with a man's calendar, but it doesn't address matters of his heart. If a career or ministry is the primary way a man experiences adventure, then chances are strong that it will win his heart over in the long run.

In a tragic irony, dedicated Christian fathers can end up raising kids that hear all about the love of their Father in heaven but see an earthly dad far more devoted to and passionate about his career and ministry than his family. As a result, many of these kids become disillusioned as they get older and turn away from their Christian faith in the process.

The fundamental problem with each of these three approaches to the "adventure vs. duty" dilemma is that they artificially separate a man's drive for adventure from his family. Adventure becomes defined as what a man wants to do, while family is what he is supposed to do. Adventure is opportunity; family is obligation. "I'd love to go back to school and get a divinity degree," confessed a dear friend, "but my kids need to have food on the table." Throwing up his hands, he concluded, "I guess every man's gotta do what he's gotta do." My friend swallowed the bitter pill of broken dreams. And, in the process, he had started to view his family as a barrier and an obstacle to his true calling.

A Summit Attempt

At the start of this chapter, I raised the question that every man asks himself: *How do I prioritize what I am driven to do with what I am responsible for?* For years, I've wrestled with a biblical response. God designs the soul of a man for adventures and exploits. In doing so, God calls him to a life of discipleship in his career and ministry (Matt. 16:24, 28:19). Yet, if a man has a family, God also calls him to be a Christlike husband (Eph. 5:23) and a spiritual leader and teacher of his children (Prov. 22:6).

We seem bent on pitting these callings against each other, like boxers in a ring. But, as long as all of them are ordained by God, they should do more than just coexist; they should actually thrive together. Each calling is meant to be a single thread, interwoven into the common fabric of a man's adventure.

Seen in this light, a man's life is not a solo climb at all. Instead, it is much like leading an Everest mountaineering expedition. Any summit attempt involves a team of climbers, several Sherpas (local hired climbers to carry supplies), and a team leader. The leader guides, protects, provides for, and, when necessary, sacrifices for his team. But, to the leader, these are more than responsibilities and chores; they are essential to the success of the expedition. An expeditionary leader can be consumed with reaching the summit, but he attains his goal by enabling his team to experience the same adventure.

When a man's life is an expedition, his family is no longer left behind at base camp while he makes a climb all by himself. Instead, his wife and children are participants accompanying him on a journey together. "Wherever you are, be all there," says missionary Jim Elliot. "Live to the hilt every situation you believe to be the will of God." When a man follows Elliot's challenge to "live to the hilt" in *every* calling of his life, then his home responsibilities no longer compete with his adventure; rather, they help fulfill it. In fact, a man pursuing dreams by himself now resembles an expeditionary leader who brazenly leaves his team en route to the summit and makes his way on his own.

This book is about becoming an expeditionary man. It's the kind of man I want to become. I've certainly not reached the summit with my family. But the five of us are outfitted with climbing gear and gradually making our way up the mountain together. En route, however, I am discovering more and more about the true ownership of the climb. It's God's expedition, not my own. As such, I've had to realign my ideas of adventure to stay on his path up the mountain. Oswald Chambers puts it like this: "I realize more and more that if we are not to forego the interests of his cross we must forego a great many other interests and how you will go, counting Christ worthy of the cost."

When a man's kids are growing up in the home, I am convinced that he cannot act upon his career and ministry aspirations in the same way as he is free to during other seasons of his life. He foregoes them. Career ambitions are placed on hold. Ministries are limited for a time. After all, a man's primary mission field is his family; it's not the outside world. His adventures must, therefore, be fully consistent with that calling, just like an expeditionary leader orients his entire venture around the climbing team.

This realignment can be tough for a man, because it means foregoing some of what naturally drives and motivates him. It also runs smack against what society—and even the church—expects of a man. But a quick read of Jon Krakauer's bestseller *Into Thin Air* will tell you that any Everest expedition led by a man with mixed agendas is doomed to failure. We shouldn't be surprised when the same setbacks and even disasters occur inside Christian homes.

"You are my greatest adventure," Bob Parr tells his family in the climax of *The Incredibles*. That line is more than lip service for the expeditionary man. It is part of God's perfect design for him. When a man lives out God's expedition rather than his own, not only will he raise spiritually healthy kids and have an ever-growing marriage, but he will also experience the godly adventure for which he so desperately yearns.

We want to hear from you. Please send your comments about this book to us in care of zreview@zondervan.com. Thank you.

ZONDERVAN.com/
AUTHORTRACKER
follow your favorite authors